Tradition and Innovation

GENERAL EDUCATION AND THE
REINTEGRATION OF THE UNIVERSITY

A Columbia Report

Tradition and Innovation

GENERAL EDUCATION

AND THE REINTEGRATION

OF THE UNIVERSITY

A Columbia Report

ROBERT L. BELKNAP & RICHARD KUHNS

Columbia University Press

New York

1977

Library of Congress Cataloging in Publication Data

Belknap, Robert L
  Tradition and innovation.

  Bibliography: p.
  1. Universities and colleges—United States—Administration.
2. Federal aid to higher education—United States.
3. Higher education and state—United States.
I. Kuhns, Richard Francis, 1924-   joint author. II. Title.
LB2341.B428   378.73   77-3315
ISBN 0-231-04322-8   ISBN 0-231-04323-6 pbk.

Columbia University Press
New York   Guildford, Surrey
Copyright © 1977 Columbia University Press   All rights reserved
Printed in the United States of America

PREFACE

We wish to thank the Rockefeller Foundation for allowing us to use its funds to help pay the costs of publishing this book, and we owe special thanks to the Carnegie Corporation for a grant to support the writing of this book, and for a subvention toward its publication.

Many of our friends and colleagues have been generous with their knowledge and their criticism. We should like to single out those who have been most directly involved with the General Education Program at Columbia as it has developed in the last three years. Carl Burton has directed, coordinated, organized, and advised on all manner of problems. Without his help we could not have written this book. Wm. Theodore de Bary more than anyone else brought together faculty, administrators, and students to reconsider Columbia's tradition of general education in the 1970s, and has offered invaluable comments on the text of this book. We are deeply grateful to Joan Turner and Cyrille White for their expert management of general education publicity, audiences, and speakers, and most especially for the editing and research assistance on which this book has relied.

R.L.B.
R.K.

CONTENTS

VII

Tradition and Innovation

Let education be conceived on right lines, let natural gifts be developed as they should, let character be formed on moral principles, and in time the effects of this will reach even to the seat of government.

Kant

⟫ INTRODUCTION ⟪

1

1   General education needs to be reconsidered

This book attacks the prevalent belief that Americans are overeducated. It argues that many, even trained professionals and powerful public figures, have resoundingly little real education. It offers a broadened vision of general education as a way to cope with this national failure and with the complacency that caused it and results from it.

Like mathematics, general education is easy to delineate through examples, but hard to define. In our atrabilious moments, we define general education as—education. Its opposite, in this context, is training. We train doctors, lawyers, historians, or physicists, but we educate human beings. We can even train animals, but we educate only human beings. Our language in its wisdom connects being human with being educable because humans have minds. Animals do not, of course, but we are concerned with another kind of mindlessness, the disease that afflicts those specialists whose training leaves them too narrow to know or care about the theory, or the history, or the impact—the human implications—of the work they do. The hard-nosed advocates of barren training have conspired unconsciously with the tender-hearted opponents of all training to drive our civilization into mindlessness. Against both these fashionable views, this book argues that education without training is impossible, but that training without education is disastrous.

Our findings reflect our reading, our discussions, and our experience at Columbia University, but many of them can serve the purposes of schools whose goals and character are very different. The American educational enterprise takes so many different forms that a book on education can only be prescriptive for a small group of schools, but can put ideas at the disposal of many. The Columbia experience is directly relevant for large, elitist, urban teaching and research institutions, but all schools are bringing their ingenuity to bear on certain common fundamental problems. The elitist schools today face external criticism and internal guilt over the vast resources they devote to the education of a few thousand people. To be at ease in the American egalitarian tradition, those who receive elitist education must perform a needed service that has wide social benefits. To train people with that scope and with some likelihood of their actually performing requires a kind of education that keeps the training we offer in the context of broad social and moral goals. Only service can justify elitist education in the long run. This preparation for service links Columbia's goals with those of most institutions.

We have been developing ways of broadening general education at Columbia University, where so much of general education started, and where it shows more vigor now than in many universities which introduced it later, such as Chicago and Harvard. Over the last three years, the Carnegie Corporation, the Rockefeller Foundation, the Mellon Foundation, and the Kenan Trust have been supporting the university's broad consideration of general education and its practical efforts to make training and education interact in the graduate and professional schools as well as in its undergraduate curriculum. In any large institution, such explorations and experiments need a forum where members of different parts of the university can exchange their ideas and learn what is going on. For three years now, we have been holding luncheons once a week where fifty or a hundred students, scholars, and administrators meet and munch sandwiches while they hear and discuss reports on problems and projects in general education. In this book we hope to share the educational ideas that have shaped and been shaped by these exchanges. In the chapters to follow we will refer to the published reports of these luncheons by volume, number, and page as, for example (*Seminar Reports* III, ii, 5).

2 American universities have changed aimlessly in response to a series of crises since World War II

Since World War II, American universities have faced a series of crises. These crises originated elsewhere but, with sad regularity, the universities responded to each in ways that made it harder to deal with the next. The first crisis came with the GI Bill of Rights, which led the private universities into an experiment in publicly subsidized education comparable to the experiment in socialized medicine being conducted at the same time by the veterans' hospitals. University enrollments rose from 1.5 million in 1940 to 2.078 million in 1946. These new students were not only more numerous, but older, more purposeful, more "upwardly mobile" than their predecessors. The universities responded to the influx by expanding their staffs and facilities. In 1945 Columbia had about 100 professors of tenured rank in the various faculties of arts and sciences; in 1950 there were some 250. In the prestigious institutions, this expansion could not meet the demand. Columbia accepted 50 percent of its applicants in the 1930s and 25 percent in 1947. The high school record for many of these students was old, and the military record had little academic meaning, so that the universities relied heavily on aptitude tests.

In 1957 the sputniks forced the universities into another kind of crisis, a crisis of national purpose. Americans realized that they had lost the technological initiative in a universally visible area, and turned to the universities to provide the training, the ideas, and often the facilities to restore our leadership in science. As instruments of American policy, the universities became politically acceptable recipients of federal funds, especially in the natural sciences. This fiscal incentive to specialize in the natural sciences, coupled with the sense that society was rewarding superiority in the natural sciences more surely and promptly than other kinds of superiority, led many of the ablest students into narrow programs of study leading directly to graduate training. To a greater degree than ever before, universities and governments became involved in one another's affairs, and universities began to think and spend like governments. In 1940, Columbia received no federal money, in 1950 $237,764, in 1960 $19.1 million, and in 1974 $78.5 million. The increase was sharper in some institutions, and constituted a larger part of the university budget in many. Money for new projects or new students seemed inexhaustible; the proliferation of administrators seemed at least harmless, and often indispensible in a community whose standards conformed more and more to those of the sources of its funds. In 1940, the Columbia address book listed no vice-presidents; in 1950 four, and in 1976 eleven.

The 1960s strengthened this working linkage between the university and the society in a rather different way. The academic social scientists raised our awareness of social inequality in America and then in many cases were recruited to devise and implement the policies to combat it. The universities themselves assumed the responsibility for providing urban studies, minority studies, and so forth—again in response to a national need that was expressed in funds for expansion. The prestigious universities found that their response to the veteran glut and the sputnik challenge had left them with a socially insensitive admissions system, based largely on aptitude scores and high school records. They worked systematically to increase the social diversity and social awareness of their student bodies, accepting some decrement in traditional knowledge and critical intellection as the proper price for social awareness and social commitment. This shift in priorities led certain high school students to cultivate social instead of intellectual activism as their best way through college admissions, eventually producing a shift in the community of students far greater than the 10-20 percent admitted under more flexible standards.

In the mid-sixties, this new student body reacted to the new vision of the university as an instrument of national policy with increasing vehemence as the nation's attention shifted from social renewal to an unsuccessful war against an enemy of another culture. The student rioters at Columbia and many other universities paid remarkably little attention to the university's educational practices. Instead, they exploited those lapses in public responsibility or public relations which seemed to implicate the university in the sufferings of the poor in our cities or the Asian countryside. The universities became the outlet for the frustrations of students impotent to produce revolution in society at large. Many universities reacted to this third crisis, a crisis of displaced drives, in a very literal manner. Some abolished grades; others liberated their students from course requirements and many of the narrower requirements for specialization; even professional schools sometimes abolished examinations. Throughout this period of relaxation, Columbia maintained these requirements and measures but devoted hundreds of thousands of man-hours to new structures of governance. The most conspicuous of these was a senate whose committees can intervene to make the university respond to social needs in awarding construction contracts, in planning personnel policies, in working with the surrounding community, and in many other areas. These responses to the crises of the late sixties cost the universities much of the money, the administrative time, the respect in the outside world, and the efficiency of centralized authority which they were to need desperately in coping with the crises of the 1970s. Before proposing our ways to break this sequence of unfortunate reactions to crisis, we shall look at several apparently separate problems that threaten once again to drive the universities to incur the wages of desperation.

3   The current financial crisis has fragmented the universities and restricted the choices open to them

Any institution would like to solve a financial crisis by increasing revenues—which is another way of saying that any institution would like not to have a financial crisis. A university draws its income from endowment, from current gifts, and from payments for its research or educational services. Forty years ago, most universities daringly shifted their endowments from bonds to equities and began living off their dividends. Ten years ago, they shifted from reliance on dividends to an endowment managed for maximal return, including capital gains. For three years, most have had capital losses instead, and many have realized that the capital gains they lived on in a time of inflation were really part of their capital. In 1955, endowment provided about 30 percent of Columbia's annual budget. In 1975, it provided 12 percent. Though other universities have high hopes of increasing their endowments by means of gifts, bequests, or the redeployment of existing capital, very few can meet sustained increases in costs with sustained increases in endowment income.

Certain universities raise millions from their alumni in annual giving campaigns. Some, including Columbia, have perhaps underrated their alumni, and should be able to increase such sums faster than inflation, but such increases bear heavy costs. Columbia University spends almost $1 million a year on its Alumni Records Center, its Office of University Development and Alumni Relations, and its College Alumni Office. It spends $300,000 more on its Office of Public Affairs, partly to make the university look worth giving to, and $200,000 on an Office of Projects and Grants that helps the different parts of the university raise funds from government and private sources.

But the hidden costs of this sort of fund-raising can be even greater. It involves university administrators with a whole constituency in addition to the students, the faculty, the staff, and the trustees. To satisfy part of this alumni constituency, some colleges use vast sums to recruit and subsidize athletes and build and maintain athletic stadiums, field houses, and coaching staffs, quite apart from any general program of physical education. Emphasis on fund-raising, moreover, may distract university administrators and alumni from other important alumni functions, such as continuing education for alumni, contact with communities through alumni, serious and frivolous encounters among alumni, and advice to the university on practical matters. Many private universities pay heavily to earn even their present alumni contributions and cannot hope to use alumni giving to abolish major deficits.

Foundations and government endowments present other problems. First, both these kinds of institution feel increasingly subject to political criticism. They hesitate to support an undertaking that may be laughed at in the Senate, knowing that the laughter may affect the next year's budget or regulations. Moreover, each administrator hopes to show to his governing board achievements that the board can use to persuade busy and potentially hostile politicians that the organization deserves support. As a result, innovation has become a central word in the fund-raising vocabulary. Many attacks on foundations contain accusations of diddling irrelevance, such as the following remark: "Foundations are . . . quiet billions, . . . administered by philanthropoids who build cuckoo clocks and try to pass them off as Cathedrals . . . building their childish sand castles on their private beaches." (Joseph C. Goulden, *The Money Givers*, pp. 317–18; quoted in Merrimon Cuninggim, *Private Money in Public Service.*)

Foundations tend to respond with language and policy that is the mirror image of such attacks: "Candidates will be required to develop and submit proposals for innovative research and/or public service . . ." or, "The decision on each research project will be based on: relevance to the questions underlying current . . . policy issues . . ."

Mere innovation, or faddishness, of course, will not produce support, but its absence will preclude it except from foundations with the courage to oppose these agents of cultural uniformity.

The emphasis on innovation means that foundations are rarely interested in supporting the later—and no longer "innovative"—stages of a program. Consequently if a university cannot perpetuate an innovation funded by a foundation or a federal endowment, the donor feels that this particular effort has failed. Often, therefore, universities cannot afford to accept proffered support, because they are already bearing the burden of too much "seed money" that sprouted.

Ⲭ The research grants and contracts for much of the scientific work follow a different pattern. These grants have led our natural scientists to expect expensive laboratories and high salaries. By and large this federal money is disbursed shrewdly, but it is not disbursed lightly. A recent grant application from Columbia Medical School contained 850 typed pages. The School of Public Health offers, in its Continuing Education program, a course on "grantsmanship." The art of grantsmanship now includes obtaining planning grants in order to be able to afford the time to make a grant application. It may seem churlish to complain about the trouble people cause in giving away money, but the complexity of the operation can have a direct effect on the history of science. In practice, an institution must write a large book to apply for a grant, and then a number of people must read that book, and years may intervene between the conception and the inception of an experiment. The resignation implicit in the following passage may be more dangerous to American scientific progress than any real funding problems:

> At present more than 2,700 papers every year refer to *nmr* (nuclear magnetic resonance). Most of these accounts appear in chemical journals. Increasingly sophisticated *nmr* experiments are being developed through improvements in instrumentation. Each new method attracts specialists who generate new descriptions of the molecules under investigation. Typically, these new methods are not quickly assimilated into the chemical community due, in great part, to the time lag between understanding the experiment and obtaining funds for the purchase of new equipment. [*Science,* 28 November 1975, p. 850]

The few great industrial laboratories, like IBM's and the Telephone Company's, have retained the capacity to react promptly which universities had when endowments were large compared with research costs. As serious as the time lag is for the progress of science, its opposite is more dangerous to the fiscal administration of universities, when they do not know, often to the very last moment, whether a grant will be available or not. A complication in an organization or in Congress can leave the university with a large ongoing operation unsupported. This danger has increased since a doctrine began to emerge among legislators and some officials that the receipt of federal money opens a university to federal supervision of activities totally unrelated to the activities for which the money was given. No law challenges an American's right to send and keep confidential letters of recommendation for students, for example, but Congress has legislated that universities which make it a policy to maintain such confidentiality may not receive federal funds. If this pattern of centralization continues, it will lead to the total shift of decision-making from those at the university who know what is going on to those in Washington who decide what should go on. The eventual answer to all these problems involving governmental contracts will be the kind of decentralization that comes with longer-term grants, allowing universities to plan staffing and research in a rational manner, to purchase equipment as the evolution of a science demands it, and to risk mistakes which they might not be able to recoup with the next year's renewal hanging over them. We expect that these changes will come, but not in time to resolve the financial crisis of the private university.

The last major source of income for the private universities is tuition. Tuition money constituted over 20 percent of Columbia's revenue in 1975. In 1965 four years at Columbia College cost about $7,700, disregarding books and living expenses. A student graduating in 1977 will have paid $14,220. At Columbia College half the students receive some scholarship aid, many have jobs, and more have loans. Except in the natural sciences, a large proportion of the graduate students are in debt. A rich university may make a plan to defer the tuition cost. Poorer universities let the student borrow from a bank to defer it. In any case, the tuition rate will not rise much faster than inflation, and any increase has educational effects which we will discuss below.

The only other way to increase tuition income is to increase enrollments. Graduate schools at the moment are trying to reduce enrollments, since they have trouble placing those Ph.D.'s they produce. Medical schools could place more graduates, but face tight constrictions on space, which they are reluctant to spend millions expanding, because increased bureaucratization of medicine may make it a less attractive profession in the next decade. Most selective colleges could expand enrollment, but largely by admitting students lower on their list of preferences than those they now admit. In certain fields such colleges could absorb more students with no problem, but in the most popular fields they would have to spend money on expansion, or reduce the amount of individual attention a student received. Because of these problems, a curious phenomenon has emerged in several universities: they want to expand, but dread the consequences.

✗ In short, most universities cannot handle the crisis of increasing costs by increasing revenues, and those that can will pay a heavy price. Without new funds, few universities can respond to rising pay scales as easily as most businesses can. Manufacturers can move to low-pay areas and postpone the problem; service industries can increase prices or tax revenues or devise procedures that use less expensive skills; and virtually every business can automate major parts of its operation to increase productivity. But productivity in a university is hard to increase, or even to define. Columbia University employs about 10,000 people full-time and gives about 7,500 degrees each year. It also produces several thousand articles, books, and learned papers a year, many of them good, and some quite important. But the fact that the average Columbia employee produces half an article and three-quarters of a degree per year proves little. A university contributes not articles but knowledge, not degrees but education and training. Administrators try to quantify this output by counting degrees or articles, or, with greater sophistication, by counting alumni listings in *Who's Who* or the footnotes that refer to a given article; but such citation studies are skewed in various ways to start with, and become more skewed as their link to funding provides incentives to distort them. We can really say only that a university like Columbia spends about $200 million a year discovering and teaching. Claims to quantify how much a university discovers or teaches are sometimes disreputable, often deluded, and invariably doomed.

✗ In the effort to behave like a business with a measurable product, a university sometimes tries to increase productivity by increasing class size. Often this works; in most subjects, with most professors, an increase from six to eight students in a group, or from seventy-five to a hundred, will make little difference, provided the physical facilities are available. To achieve such increases, however, universities are often driven to unfortunate measures, especially if the administration feels defensive about its reputation for fairness and consistency, or if it lacks the knowledge to make informed discriminations. Some universities set a bottom limit on course size; others set an average course size for a department, so that a chairman will talk about a popular course that will "float" an important one; others simply indicate that department budgets depend upon overall course enrollment. Politically, such policies protect an administration from charges of favoritism, but educationally they can be disastrous. We have seen a good midwestern university reduced to an educational shambles by the competition between departments to attract students into facile or faddish courses. More important, these students were all enrolled anyway. The tidal flow from department to department added not a cent to the university's resources.

If larger classes can be achieved selectively and wisely, they may allow a university to save money on its staff. In general, however, students remember what they say far better than what they hear or read, so that the teacher of one small class may do far more for a student's education than the teachers of several large lectures, where students remain passive. In certain fields like law, lecturers have a tradition of involving large groups actively in discussion. In fields where proper answers emerge from a less structured sequence of approximations, large lectures tend to do little more for the student than a book, except in cases where the book has not been written, or the student cannot read. Large classes, then, are not an easy solution to the problem of productivity, and at best are only a partial answer.

As an alternative way to heighten apparent productivity, universities often have students teach students, the equivalent of using less skilled labor. Many universities have tended to combine this practice with the large lecture, having scores of students listen to a lecture once or twice a week and then meet in little groups once or twice a week with section men, or laboratory assistants who are graduate students. In many cases these graduate students work very closely with the professor, receive a real education themselves in the art of pedagogy, and at the same time guide their students into making formulations and asking questions that force them to recognize new modes of thought because they are using them. In other cases, these graduate students go largely unsupervised and expend a minimum of energy on an operation which they regard primarily as a way to transfer a year's stipend from the fellowship budget of a graduate school to the teaching budget of a college. And in almost every case, these two extreme kinds of student teachers, and all those in between, are treated exactly the same by their departments; the quality of their teaching is completely ignored in the decision on whether they will teach the following year.

A second kind of graduate student teacher has full charge of a course and often a full-time job as a member of a university department. Both authors of this book started teaching as full-time instructors at Columbia while writing their dissertations. The experience was valuable, and we believe our students profited; but the hiring and rehiring of an experienced instructor deprives several other graduate students of part-time pay, and of a chance to learn to teach. At Columbia and many other institutions, therefore, undergraduates today rarely meet such experienced full-time graduate student instructors. Again, the problem is one of bookkeeping and politics. It costs a university little more to hire one student full-time and give fellowships to two than to hire three part-time, but the latter system reduces the political onus of discrimination. The hiring of less skilled instructional help, then, imposes special responsibilities upon the skilled help, and may actually be more a device to shift resources from undergraduate to graduate education than to reduce the costs of the university as a whole.

The third traditional way to reduce costs has been to speed up the educational process. When the two-year A.B. was mentioned to Woodrow Wilson at Princeton, he remarked that whoever proposed that idea had never seen a sophomore. Financially, a university would benefit little from acceleration if it charged its students by the year, but substantially if a two- or three-year degree cost the same as a four-year degree. Many medical schools recently reduced their program by a year in response to pressure from the federal agencies which helped to fund them. Such reductions did not affect the real cost of education, but simply transferred to the internship certain costs that had been part of the school years and to the residency certain costs which had belonged to the internship. In chapter 12 we will discuss the educational merits of plans to combine undergraduate and professional work; but, for financial purposes, in a world of finite annual resources for tuition payments, such plans offer little help to the universities.

If larger classes, student teachers, and speedup involve hidden educational costs in exchange for gains that are sometimes meretricious, the newer ways of increasing productivity lead to similar afterthoughts. Technology has progressed so dazzlingly that new ways of education seem obvious and benign: television, language laboratories, movies, and a multitude of teaching machines seem endlessly promising, and have tended to be just that, rarely delivering on their promise. Eventually, of course, television and movies will become a part of our armamentarium of teaching devices, just as the slide projector now is for the art historian or the natural scientist, and should be for many of the rest of us. But slides do nothing to reduce the costs; they probably do increase the productivity in an unmeasurable way—by increasing the richness and the clarity of the data pesented. Language laboratories and teaching machines offer more active possibilities, especially for independent students who want to work ahead of or apart from their class. For certain students and studies, the learning program can provide an element of play and individual challenge hard to match in class. At Columbia, and many other universities, however, most students avoid language laboratory work unless it is supervised or tested the next day by a teacher. As our tapes and programs get better, students will be using these tools more and more to supplement their books, but they will be needing their professors every bit as much, except in the acquisition of certain valuable, but essentially rote, skills. Automation may increase productivity in real education, but it will do so by improving performance, not by reducing costs.

Because the businesslike techniques for increasing productivity often fail to help the universities financially, some administrations have been driven to the mechanical reduction of academic staff. Universities across the country have tended to rank the measures they have to take, depending on the severity of the financial crisis:

1. Firing part-time instructors, to whom the university has the least legal and moral obligation.
2. Reducing or eliminating replacements for faculty members on leave.
3. Severely or completely reducing promotions to tenure.
4. Reducing or eliminating replacements for resigning or retiring faculty.
5. Eliminating certain tenure positions, or eliminating tenure.

These measures affect different communities within the university, but their overall effect is the same in every case—to reduce the diversity and the flexibility of the institution. The part-time expert brings the wisdom of another institution or a professional life to leaven the coherence of an academic community, usually for very little money. The temporary replacement enables a department to test itself against the competition and to try out new approaches or new people without making a commitment to them. The junior faculty brings the energies and the ideas to keep a university alive. If they are forbidden to associate their future with the university, and driven to expend every moment making themselves employable elsewhere, the university will have sacrificed its future identity as well as its future vigor. If a departing professor is never replaced, no departmental chairman will encourage a marginal colleague to accept another post; virtually anybody is better than nobody. And finally, any encroachment on tenure makes certain faculty reluctant to speak their minds for fear of violating the taboos of some powerful group of students, politicians, or donors to the university, since university administrators have hardly any shield but faculty tenure against the seignorial demands of individuals exacerbated by their impotence to change society as a whole. In short, many of the standard reactions to a fiscal crisis simply redistribute costs, and those that do save teaching salaries reduce a university's ability to cope with intellectual, ideological, pedagogical, or other kinds of crises.

Of course, less than half of a great university's budget pays teaching salaries. Columbia spends twelve of its $200 million on the library and the computers, and $16 million more maintaining grounds and buildings, with almost a third of that now for fuel and electricity. Money is almost as expensive as books or real estate. It takes the controller $3½ million to write 25,000 checks a month and supervise the university's spending, and it takes the personnel office and the university purchasing office another $1 million to decide what checks are written, while the treasurer, the vice-president for business, and the vice-president for fiscal management spend another $1 million taking care of the university's money in other ways. And tens of thousands of hours of professional and secretarial time go into budgets, five-year plans, financial dealings with administrators, and supervision of grants, although the salary for that time is not allocated to the fiscal budget of the university. Most important of all, perhaps, a network of underpaid secretaries and administrative assistants provides a repository of information and a communication system which enables a university to function. Few Columbia professors, for example, know how to find an empty classroom when they need one, but their administrative assistant can telephone a colleague who remembers the seating capacity of every room on Morningside Heights, and has listed in a book which ones are occupied at any hour each semester. This network costs the university several millions every year, but its efficiency would collapse if an effort to economize should sever its essential connections.

The effort to save money on nonacademic costs encounters three problems. First, the easiest things to automate offer the least rewards. A computer operating in real time, for example, could easily assign rooms, but the cost of introducing and updating data, and making it available to faculty members promptly and accurately when needed would certainly be more than now, while such data as amount of blackboard space, or accessibility to students and teacher after their last class, would almost certainly be omitted from the computer program as a frill. In such cases, the computer might save money, but it would do so by enabling an administrator to say, "The computer has all the data, and the computer says to stop pressing for a better answer; there is none"—whether there is one or not.

Universities, then, find it as hard to cut costs in areas that resemble businesses as they do in areas which differ inherently from businesses. Partly their problems involve their staff. Columbia's salary scale, for example, cannot match that of most $200 million a year businesses, and the vice-presidents in charge of a university's business have little prestige in the eyes of the faculty, and little maneuvering room for active innovation. Universities that nonetheless attract ingenious and vigorous administrators confront them with a very special kind of problem if they try to set up a system of registration, accounting, or plant maintenance that will save millions. Those millions come mostly from salaries, and campus politics aggravate the difficulties inherent in any union negotiation. Unionization at universities tends to move up the prestige ladder; once unionized, the labor force tends to be a contractually fixed cost in the university's budget, so that any savings have to come from the salaries of the nonunionized. This squeeze drives the network of secretaries and assistants to unionize, in spite of their intimate involvement in the work of their office. Once the faculty becomes the chief surviving area of budgetary flexibility, the junior faculty begins to think of unions, which drives the senior faculty to do the same despite a widespread attachment to independent professionalism and a reluctance to add a layer of union bureaucracy. Administrators look at the City University of New York, whose union won its faculty the highest salaries in the country, and willingly forego certain savings which would provoke the early stages of the unionization sequence.

We must cut costs. We cannot cut them painlessly. This economic pressure forces every part of a university to isolate and protect its enterprise. To counter the deadening effect of this defensive entrenchment, the university must enter into paradox: It must institutionalize initiative. These economic problems are not the subject of this book, but its context. They underlie certain of the intellectual, pedagogical, and political problems which we will discuss in part 2, and they set limits on the solutions which we can suggest in part 4.

⇒⇒ PROBLEMS ⇐⇐

2

4 Universities and schools have lost their common sense of what kind of ignorance is unacceptable

Quite apart from finances, our universities must find ways to handle a whole tangle of new problems, some obviously educational, and others involving larger cultural changes. In 1968, Archibald Cox looked at Columbia and wrote, "The present generation of young people in our universities is the best informed, the most intelligent, and the most idealistic this country has ever known." In the mid-seventies, that optimistic vision has collapsed. The Association of American Colleges refers casually to "the nationwide increase in student ignorance and illiteracy." The College Entrance Examination Board reports an annual decrease in scholastic aptitude scores over twelve years, and a startling number of students expect their classmates to cheat on papers and examinations. Just as Cox's optimistic vision obscures some complexities, the current pessimism affords other interpretations: the large majority of students do not cheat, but feel surrounded by cheaters; this vicarious cynicism is actually the self-definition of the adolescent idealist. The nationwide change in basic brainpower suggested by the College Entrance Board figures also can be read as a nationwide loss of those skills, habits, and awarenesses so basic and necessary that we used to equate them with intelligence. On the degree to which current students are ill-informed, however, we find clearer unanimity.

Different professors have different horror stories. A teacher of Russian needs new techniques to deal with a whole class of freshmen who do not know what a verb is. Students reading Rabelais's description of civil disturbances ascribe them to the French Revolution. A class of twenty-five had never heard of the Oedipus complex—or of Oedipus. Only one student in a class of fifteen could date the Russian Revolution within a decade. More students than ever before come to college trained in calculus, but fewer than ever before can calculate.

When university people deplore ignorance, of course, they sound like doctors bewailing the sickness that justifies their existence.

Steven Marcus challenged this pose in one of our seminars:

> There may be a certain element of cant—or of hot air—in the perennial and current lament that *the high schools in America are not doing their job. When did they ever?* Due exception must always be made historically for certain special schools both public and private, but we are speaking here about a national cultural problem that exists in similar structural configurations on a variety of levels within the system of higher education. And since a considerable part of the volume of this chorus of lamentations comes from persons like ourselves, members of the professoriat and licensed practioners of the higher pedagogical arts and crafts, I suggest that we stop bellyaching for a bit and see if we can determine what it is that we might do. One of the first things we might do is to admit that the work of higher education in America— particularly in the first two years—has varied both historically and according to what level of the system of higher education one is examining; but it has always been there. What has not always been there is the unwillingness on the part of people like ourselves to admit that this is what we are doing, and the even further unwillingness to admit that this is proper and legitimate and rewarding work for specialists in medieval literature or French history, or the logical theory of signs. If such an admission is made, then a step toward demystification among ourselves will have been taken. And if this step can be followed by the acknowledgment in all good cheer and with appropriate academic irony and skepticism—that much of the work that we have to do in the first two years is the work that is not done in secondary education and will not be done in secondary education, and that it is our proper work to do, then a step away from demoralization will have been made as well. ["Some Questions in General Education Today," *From Parnassus*: Essays in Honor of Jacques Barzun (New York: Harper & Row, 1976), p. 100]

Perhaps our entering students need not be as ignorant as Marcus says. Lionel Trilling ascribed the magnitude of our ignorance to a preventable fragmentation of the educational system:

> Among all national systems of education, the American system is unique . . . there is no intention of intellectual continuity between secondary education and higher education . . .
> The indifference of the American academic profession to the nature and quality of secondary education is supported by the attitude of advanced intellectuals and also by the attitude of the general public. [*Seminar Reports* I, iii, 2]

Over the years, this "invincible ignorance of everything that went on in secondary education," as Trilling calls it, has cut the universities off from the educational world that produces their students. Except when their own children are involved, many Columbia professors go for years without ever talking seriously with a high school teacher or with any one in Teachers College across the street. The isolation works both ways. New York, Indiana, Iowa, Oklahoma, and Oregon require virtually no college-level history courses for school history teachers. English teachers often need concepts of communication to get a job, not the ability to communicate clearly.

To prevent ignorance, colleges can influence high schools, most obviously through their admissions policies; but to do so, they should act in concert, since bad education drives out good. The most recent general change in admissions fostered ignorance in the schools in an effort to democratize the intellectual elitism of the 1950s. Those older efforts to discover an intellectual elite had already produced responses that weakened the schools. When colleges began to reject students with average grades, schools responded by raising grades and depriving their students of the distinction between good work and excellent work.

As grades reached the equivalent of Gresham's melting point, colleges began to rely on school recommendations; one town responded with archetypal idiocy; it forbade its school system to send out any unfavorable letters. Soon afterward, Senator James Buckley sponsored legislation allowing students access to their own files, which had the effect in practice of vitiating the last way schools had to reward achievement by distinguishing it from failure. As grades and letters grow bland, the colleges rely on evidence of nonacademic achievement and on the multiple-choice examinations of the electronically unimpeachable College Entrance Examination Board. But examinations resemble penicillin; the target population adjusts to them. Schools adjust their curricula to the level of understanding or the kind of answers that electrically conductive pencil marks can record. One of us returned a paper to a student with a dozen misused words underlined. When the student came for his interview, he had a brief dictionary definition for each word, and curiously, each of the defining words would have worked in place of a misused one. Finally, the student said, "You can't catch me. I memorized five thousand words before I took the college boards." He knew thousands of words, but had never wondered what a word was. Nobody had ever informed him that words aren't mechanically interchangeable, and somebody had told him always to replace a simple word with a fancy one if he could. This student had been reduced to the level of his examiners.

We are not talking about bad tests; not about the test-writer who had never encountered the word "intension," or the student who explained an excellent grade on a language examination, "I knew I couldn't read the passages; so I just figured out the answers they'd expect." We are talking about the mindlessness which the colleges unconsciously work in concert to impose on the schools by relying on multiple-choice examinations outside of the area of rote learning and mechanical problem-solving.

We agree with Marcus that colleges can cure ignorance, and with Trilling that they can prevent it; and we will show how they have done so, and how they can continue to do so. But ignorance takes many forms. It may be trivial or crucial; agonizing, unconscious, or smug. With so much to learn and so little life in which to learn it, we must select our ignorances wisely. Adolescent intellectuals often establish their corporate identity by the things they do not deign to know: "We poets need no sociology"; "We chemists pity those who never thought to prove their theories," etc., etc. And now, our universities have lost their old unanimity as to the areas of acceptable ignorance. The cult of relevance which was so modish a few years ago often concealed a mere intolerance of mental discipline, but it also sought to overcome academic ignorance of social deficiencies, everyday life, and other current matters on which the scholarly mind could throw light if it would. Within the schools this approach not only is advocated, but has become part of what is taught; the curriculum as the sanctuary of traditional bodies of lore and modes of thought has been in part replaced by the curriculum as the exposition ground for the latest literary and social experiments. Within the university itself, many students and some faculty take ignorance of certain ideas, traditions, books, and artistic monuments as evidence of independent thought. More often, they accept this ignorance of the past as the necessary price for knowledge of the present.

In any case, the modern university must find ways to deal with students whose ignorance of hard fact leads them to believe that the laws and concepts that control history are more important than the knowledge of what happened. These patterns often grow into articles of faith, of which the commonest is the simplicity of history. We have seen students traumatized to realize that a revolution could fail, or that religious periods could follow rationalistic ones, to learn that their generation was not the first to discover sexual liberty, or to encounter any other evidence against undeviating evolution. Their vague, timeless vision of a regularized past leads many of our students into an incapacity for self-conscious action which Jacob Burckhardt described:

> . . . Let us remember all we owe to the past as a spiritual continuum
> which forms part of our supreme spiritual heritage. Anything which can
> in the remotest way serve our knowledge of it must be collected,
> whatever toil it may cost and with all the resources at our disposal, until
> we are able to reconstruct the whole spiritual horizons of the past. . . .
> The only peoples to renounce that privilege are, firstly, barbarians,
> who, accepting their cake of custom as preordained, never break
> through it. They are barbarians because they have no history, and vice
> versa. They possess such things as tribal lays and a sense of the contrast
> between themselves and their enemies; these might be called the
> beginnings of history and ethnography. Yet their activity remains
> racial; it is not self-determined. The shackling of custom by symbols,
> etc., can only be loosed by knowledge of a past. [*Reflections on History*,
> New York, 1943, p. 85]

5 Our educational system isolates training from education and gives training place of honor

Our remarks about the institutional origins and cultural impact of ignorance may suggest nostalgia for a nineteenth century in which schools confidently trained students in history, calculating, English and other languages, at an age when they could benefit from and even enjoy rote learning. But even today, when we feel relatively confident about training and its goals, we are less sure about the goals of education, and least sure of the relation between training and education. Education prepares a student not for a defined career as a member of a defined group, but for a whole life as a responsible, self-conscious, and informed member of a whole society. In recent generations, we have shifted education from the crown of a student's experience to the humble beginnings of it. We pretend to derive arithmetic from set theory, to make millions of philosophers, critics, and generative grammarians who are three feet tall, but we postpone the most rudimentary knowledge of history, literature, or languages, including our own, until much later, or omit them altogether. We have turned our college into a transitional layer between sophisticated education, which is now for kids, and narrow professional training, which distinguishes the practical, working elite.

This inversion of the natural sequence can set a stamp of philistinism upon our culture as a whole. Plato's Callicles expressed the attitude millenia ago:

> Of course, Socrates, philosophy does have a certain charm if one engages in it in one's youth and in moderation; but if one dallies overlong, it's the ruin of a fellow . . . Now, my dear friend, take my advice: stop your refutations, take up the Fine Art of Business, and cultivate something that will give you a reputation for good sense. Leave all these over-subtleties to someone else. Should one call them frivolities or just plain nonsense?" [*Gorgias* 484,C-D]

We train students in something, or for something, but when we say we educate them, we feel no need to continue the sentence. Among the purest scholars, who crave precise definitions, and among budgeteers, who crave visible results, education often seems to be a luxury over which training must have priority.

But education is no luxury in our universities. Its displacement can have a very serious effect upon experts themselves. They can lose the ability to live in history, in society, and in the intellectual community as self-conscious beings. It took a literary critic to ask an excellent doctor in a Columbia seminar whether his medical advice in a certain abortion case would have been the same for a white patient as for a black patient. The doctor suddenly recognized that he had never thought about the sociology of his conduct in practice. A course in historiography can give superb technicians a totally new view of the enterprise they are engaged in. Scientists all too often consider the history, philosophy, or sociology of their fields too "soft," or relegate them to experts past their creative prime. In doing so, they isolate themselves from data which may make the difference between substantial and trivial contributions. This difference often depends on two factors—the humility to look skeptically at data which match preconceptions, and the richness of alternative conceptions which reduce the reluctance to test and abandon the initial ones. An intimate rather than a textbook knowledge of these metaspecialties which in some way or other contain or explain one's own is perhaps the ultimate mark of an educated mind.

Setting training after education can have a direct practical effect. The greatest specialists continue to educate themselves all their lives; but all too often, pedants, like adolescents, pride themselves on their ignorance of matters which could enrich their disciplines. Techniques of analysis that are commonplace in one field may remain completely unknown in another field where they are needed. Whether we are talking about Mendel's discoveries or the Xerox patent or the first play ever written in Russian, which lay unnoticed for generations in a French library, we are talking about the rarity of experts with the humility to realize and the ability to act upon the fact that they were trained in fields whose real boundaries are unknowable. The recent proliferation of "interdiscip-lines," biochemistry, economic history, psycholinguistics, socio-linguistics, comparative literature, area studies, and so forth reflects the need that scholars feel to regain some fragments of the comprehensive control that enabled the philologists and natural philosophers of other generations to grasp the world.

Outgrowing education just as the brain matures produces an unthinking professionalism which is quite distinct from stupidity. A group of architects can produce a building irreproachable in proportion and splendidly efficient for its purpose; but if its purpose is to be a gas chamber, and they ignore that fact, they have caught a disease of modern society which Hannah Arendt described:

> Except for an extraordinary diligence in looking out for his personal advancement, he had no motives at all. And this diligence in itself was in no way criminal; he certainly would never have murdered his superior in order to inherit his post. He *merely,* to put the matter colloquially, *never realized what he was doing.* It was precisely this lack of imagination which enabled him to sit for months on end facing a German Jew who was conducting the police interrogation, pouring out his heart to the man and explaining again and again how it was that he reached only the rank of lieutenant colonel in the S.S. and that it had not been his fault that he was not promoted. In principle he knew quite well what it was all about, and in his final statement to the court he spoke of the "revaluation of values prescribed by the [Nazi] government." He was not stupid. It was sheer thoughtlessness—something by no means identical with stupidity—that predisposed him to become one of the greatest criminals of that period. And if this is "banal" and even funny, if with the best will in the world one cannot extract any diabolical or demonic profundity from Eichmann, that is still far from calling it commonplace. It surely cannot be so common that a man facing death, and, moreover, standing beneath the gallows, should be able to think of nothing but what he has heard at funerals all his life, and that these "lofty words" should completely becloud the reality of his own death. That such remoteness from reality and such thoughtlessness can wreak more havoc than all the evil instincts taken together which, perhaps, are inherent in man—that was, in fact, the lesson one could learn in Jerusalem.

Of course it is important to the political and social sciences that the essence of totalitarian government, and perhaps the nature of every bureaucracy, is to make functionaries and mere cogs in the administrative machinery out of men, and thus to dehumanize them. And one can debate long and profitably on the rule of Nobody, which is what the political form know as bureau-cracy truly is. [*Eichmann in Jerusalem,* New York, 1963, pp. 287–89]

Although a majority of our students seem to select their life work sensibly, as something they can do well, can enjoy, and that needs doing, the inversion of education and training has produced one particularly sad result, the corruption of the idea of a career. Eighty percent of the students entering Columbia College intend to go on to professional school. In our Thursday Seminars, Frederick Hofmann has reviewed some of their reasons: professional salaries, security, prestige, acceptability to parents, considerable freedom to live where they please, the retention of "an individual identity in contrast to becoming, for example, an employee of IBM or General Motors," or, finally, "the recognition that admission to professional school is one of the toughest challenges facing an undergraduate today." (*Seminar Reports* III, iii, 30–31) Dr. Hofmann describes one frustrating interview where the student finally blurted out, "Gosh, Doctor, I can't answer your questions—I've been so busy concentrating on how to get into medical school that I haven't had time to think about what a physician's life is like."

The tremendous costs of education, coupled with a diminished number of positions at each step in a student's career, has produced a desperate competitiveness. Lowell Bellin described this pressure at another of our Thursday Seminars:

After World War II, it was hard for even "the best and the brightest"— however they were defined in those days—to get into medical school. Few of the aspirants dared miss any bets. Before enrolling in any specific college course, we customarily scrutinized every medical school catalogue we could lay our hands on. These catalogues inevitably communicated a utilitarian calculus that directed our selection of undergraduate courses. We premedical students were desperate. We lacked pride. We were pathetically anxious to please. It was a seller's market, and we premedical students were assuredly in no position to bargain.

We were informed that American medical schools now preferred that premedical students major in the humanities. No longer would American physicians be known exclusively as vocationalists. Instead, in the tradition of Osler, future American physicians would be broad-gauged intellectuals at home in the world of philosophy, history, and the other humanities, as well as in the sciences.

Did we premedical students disapprove of this policy?

Hardly. Few of us really objected to any proposition calling for our semi-immersion in the humanities. To us, the humanities were relaxing. It was practically always easier to get an honors grade in a humanities course than in zoology, chemistry, or physics courses. Understandably, we came to look upon the humanities as a means to elevate our academic average. And our overall academic average in college would be enormously important to survive the eventual unsentimental screening process of the medical schools.

But things were not what they seemed. Analysis of their catalogues suggested to us that the pro-humanities polemics on the part of the medical schools were verbal moonshine designed to mesmerize the unwary into taking courses irrelevant to medical school admission. [*Seminar Reports* III, vii, 136–37]

This transformation of an education into an admissions procedure and a university into a way station affects those students most pathetically who most need real education. The vicarious terrors or ambitions of their parents drive them to live like some futuristic Jack. They attend a kindergarten that will get them into a school that will get them into a college that will get them into medical school that will get them a practice that will enable them to build up an estate that will support them in style in the finest cemetery Florida can provide.

At one point, some of us thought this problem could be solved by exporting, to the benighted purveyors of the technical, that understanding of values which lay at the center of the humanities. We soon learned that the professional schools felt little need for the missionary services of a band of "value technicians" who would come and civilize them. They felt rather that a series of historical accidents, such as the Flexner report in medicine, had isolated certain integral parts of human experience as professions while leaving others as "proper" subjects for pure scholarship and undergraduate study. At one of our seminars, Telford Taylor discussed this need for reintegration of the university in historical terms, observing that the isolation of the law schools has withdrawn law

as a staple subject in the arts and sciences curriculum. To be sure, there are courses in constitutional law; there are quite a few other courses of a legal or quasi-legal nature but, in the undergraduate curriculum, these courses— unlike those in such fields as history, economics, political science, languages—have not been assembled in a discipline as a focus for a major in a departmental organization. That, of course, is quite contrary to the structure on the other side of the Atlantic. Many, many students who go to British universities take law the way they might otherwise take history or economics, and they use it as the focus of their liberal arts training, without the slightest intention of becoming professional lawyers after graduation. That isn't at all possible here. . . .

That is an important minus in the structure we have evolved. . . . Law has very close relations to political science, to literature, and to philosophy; it is, as it were, the matrix of the organizational side of society. It has overtones in many directions. . . . We should move in the direction of putting back into the undergraduate curriculum the idea of law, its nature and sources, and some of its practical applications. . . . In our own law school curriculum, this focus on the professional aspect has tended to make it over-professional. It seems to me most unfortunate the way that, in all law schools—and ours is no exception— legal history has tended to fall very close to the bottom of the list of subjects that students pursue with some interest. As a result, they now get a rather insufficient notion of the sources of law. I also think it unfortunate that courses such as jurisprudence, where the philosophical implications of law are dealt with, are being slighted. And I think that here, again, we see the results of an almost exclusive emphasis on the professional aspects of the legal education. [*Seminar Reports* I, vi, 5, 8]

James Polshek, Dean of the School of Architecture, described a very particular kind of damage done by the isolation of the professional school:

There has developed during [the] evolutionary process a lack of criticality on the part of the profession. And so, as far as we at the school, and most enlightened architects are concerned, the profession cannot reform itself. This reform can only take place, it seems to me, within the university; and it can only take place—it seems to me— within a university such as this, where the particular node of the

> university, [in this case, our school] can be enlightened and informed by
> those other forms of education that are simultaneously taking place.
> [*Seminar Reports* I, vii, 1]

Here, then, is the proper use for a great university: to provide the cross-criticism that can force narrow groups to bring their minds to bear afresh upon problems about which they have become complacent. Mitchell Ginsburg, Dean of Columbia's School of Social Work, gave one of our seminars an example of the dangers of compartmentalized professional thinking. He discussed

> the need for various disciplines to work together . . . the need for
> research and evaluation is clear. I would offer the warning, however,
> that major social policy decisions are never made solely on the basis of
> research findings. . . . Thus, a whole series of recent research studies
> points out quite clearly that most people on welfare have a strong
> commitment to the work ethic, and that the development of elaborate
> work training programs and compulsory work requirements is
> unnecessary. From a cost-benefit point of view, they defeat the purpose,
> and, therefore, in a logical policy framework, should not be included.
> But it is politically necessary, and nobody in Congress would consider
> supporting a bill without features of that kind included, even though the
> Secretary of HEW has gone on record indicating that it is going to cost a
> lot of money and not do any good. I would hope that if one looks at this
> whole area of social policy there might be some way that a university,
> particularly through its general education program, would make it
> possible for representatives of students and faculties from the various
> professions and disciplines to work together on some of these key
> issues. [*Seminar Reports* II, ii, 6]

Our professional training is often crippled by our failure to bring the entire accumulated force of scholarly tradition to bear upon the professions. At one of our Thursday Seminars, we heard a man who had been both a minister of education and a major figure in diplomacy. In his talk, "Education for Diplomacy," Abba Eban made it clear that for diplomacy, professional training, in the narrow sense, may presuppose a knowledge of the future which we do not have:

> Diplomacy is regarded like economics, like mathematics, like
> engineering, like dentistry, as something that requires a specialized

understanding: namely, the concentration of a searchlight on a very narrow area in order to elicit all its mysteries. I don't believe that that is the correct approach and I think that the traditional emphasis on a general education, with an emphasis perhaps on history—that is to say, a discipline in which nations do emerge as the primary theme—*that* I think should be the first concomitant. Of course, there are problems of law and of economics that arise. The study of war and peace, deterrence and miscalculation, disarmament—all of these are bound to arise in a diplomat's life. But it is impossible to predict, in the present rhythm of change, on what the diplomatic attribute will have to be focused.
[*Seminar Reports* II, ii, 1]

The barriers between our colleges and our professional schools will not, of course, simply disappear. A professional possesses special knowledge and skill. When Columbia's Psychoanalytic Institute opens major courses to a psychohistorian or a Dostoevsky specialist, it must make very sure those specialists will use what they learn as scholars, not as healers. Professions used to be called mysteries, and certain skills must necessarily remain esoteric. But this practical training in a profession surprisingly seldom entails ideas and methods that are inexplicable, ineffable, or beyond the grasp of a genuinely educated layman. True experts seek ways to communicate. Pseudoexperts rely on the secrecy of their data for their place in society, claiming that disclosure of their secret lore would make them helpless, when, actually, it might only show them to be useless. Here, what was once a mystery becomes a mystification.

6   We also isolate the disciplines from one another

Departments in the arts and sciences are often as isolated from any university community as are the professional schools. A teacher of eighteenth-century literature may work twenty years at Columbia before he meets a certain teacher of eighteenth-century history. Graduate students often dare not steal an hour from their study of Russian literature to hear a lecture by one of the world's experts on Russian art. Although the central faculty of most universities is called the Faculty of Arts and Sciences, the most extreme isolation prevails between the experts in the arts and the experts in the sciences.

A remarkable number of scientists delight in music and know the arts in general, while operating in total ignorance of the studies their colleagues are making of these materials. Few scientists will confuse a fondness for alcohol with an understanding of organic chemistry, but many confuse a fondness for Shakespeare with an understanding of literary analysis, and imagine that their colleagues are hired to sit around enjoying Shakespeare or musing about Hannibal. At one of our Thursday Seminars, this scientific vision of other disciplines emerged as follows:

> . . . we try to give even freshman students some exposure to the essential method by which scientists discover "truths." If I may simply describe the essence of the method here, there are two special features to it: When a scientist in some way becomes aware of a fact for which there is no existing satisfactory explanation, his first impulse is to try to devise an attractive explanation which is satisfying both intellectually and esthetically; having done this, he has the immediate obligation to try as hard as he can to prove that his explanation is wrong. In general, scientific explanations are not proven—they simply survive all real efforts to disprove them. Attempts at disproof in general involve the use of controls. To give an example in a non-scientific area, if one were convinced that the potential competition of the German Navy for superiority on the seas had been a major contributor to the origin of the First World War, one would simply reconstruct all the circumstances again omitting this competition, and see if a war did indeed occur.
>
> This example illustrates not only the great advantage scientists have in being able to run controlled experiments in which variables can be selectively tested but also how difficult it is in many other fields to get the same kind of information. [*Seminar Reports* I, iv 3]

In the humanities, on the other hand, most scholars are acutely aware of their ignorance of scientific scholarship. They do not delight in the subject matter of the natural sciences, but they stand in awe of the techniques used and the special languages adopted by their scientific colleagues. Historians have quantified their inquiry, structuralist literary scholars have geometricized their study of texts, and everywhere in the humanities the thirst for scientific certainty exceeds the comprehension of science. Very few scholars in the humanities can read and write the language of science, which is mathematics. If they did master that language, as they did in earlier generations, they might be more realistic in their attempts to adopt an alien methodology.

The nonscientists have cut themselves off from this tool partly because they lack the time to learn mathematics, and partly because they have been terrorized by school and college science teachers. As researchers, natural scientists "pursue the truth in packs" but, as teachers, even the very best of them tend to work alone, so that no tradition of teaching has emerged. Most college science courses, therefore, consist of lectures by a professor, administering incontrovertible data to a multitude, whose active work consists of problem-solving to show and develop manipulative capacities.

Students who love science or who see a doctor's career behind it will accept such training. Many of those who go on into research describe a real shock when called on to ask a question and design an experiment that will answer it. Their college training had prepared them for this aspect of science by ignoring it. Nonscientists, of course, have no use at all for problem-solving techniques in thermodynamics. Some want patronizing courses, "Rocks for Jocks," taught by a benign geologist; and some want faddish courses, "Ecology and Ethology," or "The Psychology of Ideology"; but scientists as well as nonscientists need courses that will force the students to do some real scientific thinking without having mastered the techniques a modern scientist needs. We will suggest ways in which universities can lead their scientists to make this kind of thinking available to students with ambitions in the sciences, and the other fields.

For every scientist who reads *PMLA* (Proceedings of the Modern Language Association), there are several teachers of humanities who read *Science* regularly, and wish that some time in their college career someone had given them a hint that science is a real intellectual activity. Years after all those hours spent in making sure equations came out right, or picking up little weights with tweezers in rituals that once had meant something, a few historians or poets, late in life, by chance learn that science is not a body of formulas and a set of experimental rituals that function like Tibetan prayer wheels, but an ongoing activity of the human mind, with scholars setting problems and testing solutions to them just as in their own fields. A scattering of scholars in the humanities finds this out about science, but hardly a scientist discovers this about the humanities.

In the modern university, the humanities are isolated from the sciences and the professions, but the various fields within the humanities are also isolated from one another. We have discussed the causes of this isolation and will discuss ways of dealing with it.

In the traditionally organized centers of scholarship, the sharpest break within the humanities separates the teacher of a creative art from the scholar: a teacher of painting or acting has embarrassingly little contact with a teacher of art or theater history. Unlike the professions of law and medicine, which have been pulled out of the university arts and sciences curricula, fields such as acting and painting are split between the practical and the scholarly, with only the most enlightened schools actively fostering the contact between the two. In chemistry, most teachers assume that undergraduate students cannot approach the theory without using their hands in the laboratory, but most professors of art history regard practical experience in the studio as an interesting, enlightening, humbling, but essentially irrelevant activity for their students. This separation from the practicalities of artistic activity leaves students in the humanities unable to deal with many works of art except in unrealistic and abstract terms. It also isolates students of acting, painting, and the other studio and performing arts from the magnificent structures of intellection which should be enriching their performances. The most creative and most interesting scholars often rise above this artificial distinction. The scholars who control the arts and sciences curricula feel that the practical arts courses disregard the rigorous development of intellectual skills. The practitioners of the arts, realizing that their work is ontologically prior to and as rigorously demanding as scholarly work, want to remove the distinction between their courses and the rest of the curriculum. As long as arts courses are mere electives, the charges of indiscipline will very often be justified. Where an area of study is set up which establishes a rigorous prerequisite for any advanced course, and culminates in auditions or exhibitions in a professional context, students and faculty take courses in the arts as seriously as in the rest of the curriculum.

The universities themselves are thus as guilty in isolating scientists, scholars, and artists as they are in isolating professionals from the community with which they will have to work. This isolation denies all these groups intellectual existence outside of their careers, although their emotional and aesthetic life may remain much broader. Within these isolated professions the patronizing attitude toward outsiders becomes increasingly hard to avoid. Specialization in recent decades has made the old divisions of knowledge and the old careers even narrower and more excluding, with a consequent reduction of the number of people with whom the specialist feels any solidarity. This intellectual fragmentation has made it virtually impossible for universities to function as social units.

7 **This educational disintegration works together with other social and intellectual trends to produce a widespread mindlessness**

The misplaced emphasis on career training and the isolation of the professions have produced a pair of effects which every teacher has seen in class. The first effect emerges in the students who dare not make any statement at all on a given subject because they are not experts on it. Such people are the destined victims of false experts. The second effect emerges in those students who believe that anything they say sincerely is true. Much modern school teaching encourages this belief out of a fear of discouraging the free flow of creativity. These two forms of mindlessness reflect one another. By neglecting their intellectual contact with the untrained majority of humanity, our experts have driven that majority into a dim realm where, as nonexperts, they cannot think, but only feel.

In its worst manifestations, this cult of sensibility kills thought; in its best, it calls us back to the values and attitudes which professional careerism has submerged. Gerald Else has written a defense of feeling and a warning against its loss in an education expressed in abstractions, but feeling in his sense disappears equally dangerously in the face of feeling as an arbiter, a judge, a private response unrelated to the responses of others and unmonitored by any cognitive standards or investigations concerning reality. Else is defending appropriate feeling against an artificial distrust of intuition; scientistic deprecation, Else argues, has reduced our affective lives from the educated responses of experienced minds to mere subjectivity validated by authentic feeling. ("Some Ill-Tempered Reflections on the Present State of Higher Education in the United States," *Daedalus*, Fall 1974, pp. 138-42.)

The proper use and understanding of affect remains as much a problem in the undergraduate colleges as it does in the professional schools. The unwillingness and the inability to cope with feeling in undergraduate work has its consequences later on when the profession usurps all of the students' energies. Then, the difficulties of dealing with feeling can be "overcome" by denying that feeling belongs at all in professional expertise. We create a cohort of scientifically precise, affectively an-aesthetic creatures. The failure to respond to *King Lear* or *Oedipus* suggests the kind of emotional frigidity which is often ascribed to terror. A college student's anxiety over his inability to say or feel the right thing may be so strong that he cannot feel anything. Education should not teach such students to emote, but rather give them confidence in their ability to cope with complex emotional situations and release their natural responses to these works. The cultivation of affective response as part of the concern of education can undermine that gratifying insulation from suffering which enables a surgeon or a welfare economist to function, but it can also lead them to prevent avoidable suffering, which they might otherwise ignore.

This disjunction between feeling and intellection is part of the same complex of problems that we have been describing: the loss of unanimity about ignorance, the fragmentation of the intellectual world, and the loss of social solidarity. Many social critics have offered explanations for these problems. Some have suggested that young people today form their consciousness through television which is not only repetetive and set at a density of allusion and intellection that will elude as few listeners as possible, but also offers fewer choices than a library and is harder to skim. Others ascribe it to parents who witheld their guidance and example in the face of scary and half-comprehended doctrines on child-rearing. Others ascribe this complex of problems to the undermining of the foundations of certainty by Gödel, Heisenberg, and Einstein. Still others point out that Marx and Freud offer a new variant on the old *ad hominem* disputation which enabled people to explain an argument away without ever confronting its points. Some historically oriented critics point out that the hydrogen bomb threatened the deferral of gratification on which long-range thinking eventually depends; while others note that America without striving or consideration had tumbled terrifyingly from the poverty and impotence of the thirties into the riches and power of the sixties. The scholars at Columbia have led us to be acutely conscious of our historical need to come to terms with important elements of this complex. Richard Hofstadter's enormous study of anti-intellectualism in American life localizes a problem which Lionel Trilling's book on authenticity traced to European romanticism. In considering American cultural documents, Quentin Anderson has merged these two strands of thought in his book on the imperial self.

Without denying any of these explanations, we would content

ourselves with observing a crisis in our whole culture. Faiths are shaken, and universities can only play a little part in determining whether our civilization will weather the crisis somewhat changed or be replaced by something unimaginable. No act of will can frame the doctrinal and social syntheses we need. The universities can only do two things: educate the thinkers and the doers who will decide our future, and provide a locale for some of them in which opposition takes the form of intellectual onslaught instead of ignorance, oppression, or blind rejection. The rest of this book will describe how the universities can work towards this end.

3

8 Between the two world wars, Columbia established courses to introduce college students to Western culture

Columbia had a long tradition of self-conscious curriculum planning to confront the problems we have described, including programs that stimulated educational changes in schools of very different character, sometimes by imitation, sometimes with adaptations to local needs, and sometimes through the kind of adverse reaction that leads to educational diversity. We have been trying to continue this tradition of educational exploration. At one of our Thursday meetings, Lionel Trilling described the historical and institutional circumstances that generated this curricular thinking at Columbia:

> I'll begin my summary account of the history . . . at Columbia with the year 1889 and the deliberations of the Trustees over whether or not it was expedient to abolish Columbia College. In those days we were not yet incorporated as a university even though in effect we were one, and what had once been called and now is called Columbia College was referred to as the "School of Arts" or as the "College proper." The idea that our undergraduate college with its commitment to liberal education stood in the way of the right development of the institution as a whole had been proposed by the President, Frederick A. P. Barnard. In the event, his view was rejected—the Trustees, on the motion of their chairman, Hamilton Fish, resolved that it was *not* expedient to do away with the "College proper."
>
> The matter wasn't by any means settled with the passing of this resolution. In 1876 the Trustees had invited John W. Burgess to fill the Chair of History, Political Science, and International Law; there were big chairs in those days and presumably men big enough to fill them. It was understood that Burgess was to develop graduate study here at Columbia according to the model of the German universities. He had studied at Goettingen, Leipzig, and Berlin, working under the best professors of the great German historical school. He was to establish here the ethos and the methods of these preeminent scholars, their commitment to the ideals of modern science. This being his mission, it was inevitable that Burgess should have directed toward the antiquated ideals of the undergraduate college an unremitting antagonism.
>
> It can't be said that the contempt in which Burgess held the College, and to which he presumably recruited the opinion of President Barnard, was wholly unjustified. At the time, when Burgess came upon the scene

and for a good many years thereafter, the "College proper" was a small old-fashioned school, its curriculum limited to Latin, Greek, mathematics of an outmoded sort, a little metaphysics, a very little natural science. Burgess saw it as kept in being only by inertia and the piety of its alumni. In his view the one thing that might rationalize its existence would be its consenting to limit itself to what he called a "gymnastic" function—that is, to do the work of a German *Gymnasium*; giving the pupils, by drill and rote-learning, the tools they would need as postulants either of pure scholarship or professional practice.

In 1894 the "College proper" found its champion, and Burgess met his legendary opponent, in John Van Amringe, who in that year was appointed Dean of the College. For Van Amringe no claims of intellectual distinction can be made. He had wanted to be Professor of Latin and Greek in the College, and when that ambition was frustrated, he accepted the professorship of mathematics. In both fields he was a sincere scholar of no originality whatever. He seems to have had no particular respect for intellectual achievement and to have favored athletes over serious students. But he thought that the "College proper" did an important thing—the College, he said, did a job of "making men."

Given Van Amringe's intellectual temperament, given, too, his social class as a member of an old Knickerbocker family, and his personal disposition, which was perhaps too much on the clubbable and convivial side, there is some reason for surprise that he meant what he really did mean when he talked about "making men."

Actually the import he gave to that depressing phrase was anything but petty and merely moralistic. When he spoke of the College "making men," he meant that it did not concern itself to make specialist-scholars or practitioners of the professions, but that it aimed to teach them to look before and after, and in general to use their minds in ways which are appropriate to civil existence. In all his annual reports Van Amringe asserted his belief that this aim was forwarded by liberal undergraduate education, and he resisted all efforts to curtail its scope.

Of such efforts there were many during the term of Van Amringe's service as Dean of the College and despite his resistance they were mostly successful. In the early years of this century the idea of the undergraduate college fell into disrepute with many serious Americans. Some decades earlier the tendency had gone the opposite way and the professional schools of the first rank had insisted upon graduation from college as a requirement for admission. Now this came to be thought supererogatory and even harmful. In 1902, Nicholas Murray Butler, in his presidential report, expressed his belief that "four years is too long a time to devote to the College course as now constituted, especially for students who are to remain in University residence as technical or professional students." And in his report of 1903, President Butler advocated that there be set up in the College a two-year course as an option along with the usual four-year program. In 1905 he was able to announce with pride the establishment of the plan of "professional option," the so-called "Columbia plan" by which a student after two years of College might go on to one of the University's professional schools.

Butler summed up the meaning of the new arrangement in the following words: "The Faculty of Columbia College say explicitly that to prescribe graduation from a four year college as a sine qua non for the professional study of law, medicine, engineering, or teaching is not to do a good thing but a bad thing."

Why was it not a good thing but a bad thing? Butler was in no doubt about the reason. In those days what we now call liberal education went under the name of "culture" and Butler said flatly that "any culture that is worthy of the name . . . will be increased, not diminished, by bringing to an end the idling and dawdling that now characterize so much of American higher education."

Idling and dawdling: it makes a harsh indictment. But the winds of educational doctrine are never steady; perhaps they don't blow as they list, but, rather, at the behest of all sorts of social circumstances, including the supply and demand of the labor market; yet this assures that they never blow for long from the same direction. No sooner had "idling and dawdling" been curtailed by cutting down the number of college years through "professional option" than Butler began to wonder whether he after all quite liked the new efficiency. In his report of 1909, he offers dark reflections on what he calls "the cult of the will," which, he says, "has gone far enough just now for the good of mankind." Suddenly, it seems to him that young men are in much too much of a hurry to become lawyers, doctors, engineers, teachers; and he reflects nostalgically that the four-year undergraduate college did after all make possible what he now calls the "generous and reflective use of leisure." [*Seminar Reports* I, iii, 1–2]

In the atmosphere described by Trilling, a group of Columbia professors decided that their freshmen lacked the cultural and intellectual background to respond responsibly to the political and ideological challenge of World War I. To deal with this ignorance the professors of that day set up a course in Contemporary Civilization which they described in the 1919 college catalogue as follows:

> The aim of the course is to inform the student of the more outstanding and influential factors of his physical and social environment. The chief features of the intellectual, economic, and political life of today are treated and considered in their dependence on and difference from the past. The great events of the last century in the history of the countries now more closely linked in international relations are reviewed, and the insistent problems, internal and international, which they are now facing are given detailed consideration. By thus giving the student, early in his college course, objective material on which to base his own judgment, it is thought he will be aided in an intelligent participation in the civilization of his own day.

The second year the course was given, the last sentence of this description was amended to read:

> To give the student early in his college course objective material on which to base his own further studies and his own judgment will, it is believed, aid him greatly in enabling him to understand the civilization of his own day and to participate effectively in it. [Quoted in *A History of Columbia College on Morningside*, New York: Columbia University Press, 1954, p. 100]

Then, as now, every Columbia College student had to take this course. There were no lectures; two dozen different teachers from many departments met with small groups of students four times a week to discuss a fixed list of readings. Justus Buchler described the three guiding questions in these discussions as follows: "How have men made a living? How have they lived together? How have they interpreted the world they lived in?" (*ibid.*, p. 102) Buchler goes on to describe the readings in the early days:

> From the beginning CC [Contemporary Civilization] has based itself largely on materials written or edited by members of the staff: a carefully wrought educational venture needs specially devised instruments. . . . In those days, when you were requested to do a piece for CC you found yourself doing it; you couldn't resist, and anyhow, you had always wanted to do something like it—that's why you were collaborating in a new enterprise.

The compendia of original documents and historical articles published by the Contemporary Civilization staff remain a major force in college education to this day. (See appendix 2.) Buchler justified this kind of course as follows:

> The Columbia College experience testifies that journalistic simplifications and excessive temporal closeness to the scene make critical understanding of the present virtually impossible. It is the present, the trends of contemporary society, that need the benefit of clarifying perspective. The gross currents of the present the student already possesses when he first turns, as he does today in CC, to an examination of the medieval heritage. In first being guided to the historical framework of the present, he has the detachment necessary for objectivity and receptivity. It is, of course, as difficult for him to identify with the past as it is for him to detach himself from the present. But to attempt the former is a greater initial challenge to his imagination. When he begins the second year of CC he has not only gained sufficient scientific detachment for the more analytical study that is to deal with contemporary society, but he can be both more critical and more constructive than he would otherwise be, because he is less gullible and more historical minded.

In the 1930s the Columbia faculty became aware of another set of problems much like those afflicting universities today. Again, these problems centered upon ignorance, and another general course, called Humanities, was added to the required curriculum. Humanities, a year course, meeting as CC did, four times a week in small groups, was devoted to reading some ten to a dozen "great books" each term. The reading ranged over the major works of the West, from Homer to Goethe and, in later years, to Dostoevsky. This course resembled CC in its effort to remedy certain kinds of ignorance, but the nature of its subject matter made it depart from CC in the kinds of understanding which it set out to encourage.

The idea of general education flourished, not only in the required courses we have described, but in upperclass seminars to which admission was granted to only the very ablest students.

The junior-senior Colloquium, as it was called, drew celebrated faculty from the humanities departments, and students from all disciplines. Acceptance to the two-year sequence was by letter of recommendation and interview. Most students stayed the two years, working in groups of 12 to 15 with two instructors from separate disciplines. (See appendix 1 for syllabi.)

Though established some twenty years apart, CC and Humanities and the Colloquium answered needs of the student in the United States who had not had the benefits of a *lycée* or *gymnasium* education, on the one hand, and who, as citizens of a democracy in which they were presumed to participate, had an obligation to be knowledgeable about political matters, and analytical in the handling of cultural problems. In short, CC and Humanities were designed to fit the specific needs of undereducated and presumably fully participating citizens of a democracy. CC and Humanities were answers to both educational and political problems. These courses, which Columbia pioneered between World War I and World War II, strengthened American education in its breadth and individuality. Similar courses were adopted at dozens of colleges throughout the country.

9 For two decades after World War II this system developed and flourished

Unanimity has rarely oppressed Columbia, but by mid-century most of those concerned took pride in the college curriculum. Constant intercourse with skeptics had led the practitioners of general education, not only to elaborate the original coherence of purpose into a sophisticated rationale, but also to keep adjusting to the times and to the diverging needs of different groups within the university. CC in the twenties, and Humanities in the forties, had expanded into two-year sequences, and the program had become central in the college curriculum. In this chapter, we shall discuss the impact of this mature system of general education.

Every freshman entered Columbia College knowing that half of the forty courses he would take in his eight semesters would be required for his general background, and half of the remaining courses for his major. Whether he aspired to a career in law, medicine, poetry, or astrophysics, a student knew that he and all his classmates would take the following courses:

	No. semesters	No. Classes per week	No. credits
Ideally in freshman year:			
Contemporary Civilization A	2	4	8
Humanities A	2	2	8
Freshman English	1	2	2
Physical Education	4	2	8
Ideally in sophomore year:			
Music Humanities	1	3	3
Art Humanities	1	3	3
Contemporary Civilization B	2	3	6
Natural Science or Math	4	3 or 4	16
Language	6	3 or 4	24

Total: 68 to 78
(out of a total of 124 credits)

Except in modern languages, virtually none of the students could fulfill these requirements in high school. The existence of these requirements tended to exclude those students who had already narrowly defined their plans for life, and also those who hoped to survive college on easy courses.

Any school whose students are being driven to substitute training for education can use such an array of requirements to free students from the narrowing pressure of parents, peers, and professional schools. Paradoxically, requirements can liberate.

Columbia administrators and faculty members often considered an alternative system of lectures and tutorials; this would offer the advantages of economy for the university and wide contact with major figures for the students. The course staffs and the majority of the faculty always rejected such proposals on pedagogical and administrative grounds. Pedagogically, they believed that Columbia freshmen learned from what they said, not what they heard, that the introductions to university study should involve the active, and not the passive use of the mind. Administratively, they were certain that senior faculty would be reluctant to participate in such courses as mere section men, and that a group of junior staff subordinated to a single lecturer would offer less enthusiasm and hard work than they would as full members of a rather distinguished teaching company.

In practice, the teaching staff of Humanities and CC may have been a more important educational invention than the curricula of these two courses. Membership in this staff mobilized energies and provided an education in pedagogy which senior and junior colleagues could never have encountered in any other way. Peter Gay has caught the mood of the staff in this period:

> When I first began teaching CC,—first CC A and then several times CC B—in the late 1940s, it was something of a Deweyite (or shall I say, dewey-eyed?) Common Faith. Those of us in CC A taught 11 hours a week instead of the customary 9 without complaining. We attended our Thursday lunches with obsessive regularity, and if someone was away it meant that he was sick. We earnestly debated individual selections and even the wording of examinations as though salvation depended on the right choice. [*Seminar Reports* I, v, 1-2]

Morale is catching, and most new members of these staffs acquired an involvement that they in turn passed on to their students. A generation of students took masochistic pride in the immense reading lists, and turned the course into a rite of passage in which they achieved their manhood through the rigor of their intercourse with their intellectual ancestors.

Columbia in those days confronted many of the problems which many universities confront today. Certain students brought from their high schools a heritage of ignorance every bit as rich as the heritage they bring today. But more important, almost all of them brought from their background a drive to succeed in the professional world which tended to narrow their outlook in much the same'way as careerism today narrows students' outlook. The general education requirements, as few administrators recognized, were already beginning to function as a liberating educational instrument. Students forced to take Humanities and CC could work secure in the confidence that their classmates were not winning the race by taking premedical neurophysiology instead.

In Contemporary Civilization, the entire population of Columbia College encountered selections from important works of the distant and recent past gathered into four volumes which have been used in similar courses around the country ever since. In Humanities, the students read a major classic every week or two in its entirety. This breakneck speed demands able and excited students, and even with them, it laid these courses open to charges of "tourism," dilettantism, or outright irresponsibility. To answer these charges, the staffs said that the serious conduct of the class demands juxtapositions, sequences, and direct encounters with a variety of major texts. Teachers who are experts on only one of these texts can master enough of the scholarship on the others to bring their background to bear on them for brief periods, and can share the students' exploration of unknown territory in a way that will make that exploration intellectually respectable. Arthur Danto expressed a more theoretical justification for this speed:

> If there were only one work of art in the world, our artistic responses to it would be far more meager than if there were two works, assuming we knew the two works. For we could not see the artistic differences between this work and any others, and being artistically different from B is an important fact about A. In this sense, readers of Virgil were in a better position to appreciate Homer than were Homer's contemporaries, and that entire audience which existed in the interval between Homer and Virgil. Works of art form a class with the following property: Each addition to it enriches the members so that, in an important sense, art revolutionizes art, and a work of art is a different object after another work of art has been created, than it was before then. Essentially the same may be said of our *experiences* with works of art. Strictly, one has not fully experienced Homer until one has experienced Virgil. Strictly, indeed, so long as it is possible for there to be new works added to the class of art works, one has not *fully* experienced any work of art. The more works we experience, the richer our experience of any one of them. The limit on the number of works to be experienced in our course is determined only by the limits of a student's capacity to absorb and relate. A course which considered a work a day, assuming a capacity far

in excess of what is realistic to assume, would be not merely a *quantitatively* richer course than one which considered only one work a month. In contrast with a prevailing aesthetic, *more* is *more*.

Still, the reading lists were formidable. For example, in 1951-52, all the following books were required:

Homer: *Iliad*
Aeschylus: *Prometheus Bound; Oresteia*
Sophocles: *Antigone; Oedipus Rex; Philoctetes*
Euripides: *Medea; Hippolytus; Bacchae*
Aristophanes: *Clouds; Frogs*
Herodotus: *The Persian Wars* (selected books)
Thucydides: *History of the Peloponnesian War*
Plato: *Apology; Crito; Euthyphro; Symposium; Republic*
Aristotle: *Ethics; Poetics*
Lucretius: *On The Nature of Things*
(The Bible): Job
Virgil: *Aeneid*
Saint Augustine: *Confessions* (Books 1-10)
Dante: *Inferno*
Rabelais: *Gargantua and Pantagruel* (Books 1 and 2)
Montaigne: *Selected Essays*
Cervantes: *Don Quixote*
Shakespeare: *Henry IV; King Lear*
Milton: *Paradise Lost*
Spinoza: *Ethics* (Books 1-3)
Molière: *Misanthrope; Tartuffe; School for Wives*
Swift: *Gulliver's Travels*
Voltaire: *Candide; Zadig and Micromégas*
Goethe: *Faust (Part 1)*
Rousseau: *Confessions*
Lessing: *Laocoön*
Nietzsche: *Beyond Good and Evil*
Blake: *The Portable Blake*
Dostoevsky: *Crime and Punishment*
Shaw: *Man and Superman*

Since 1969, the last few weeks of the course have included books drawn from this list, plus some more modern works, selected individually by each instructor after discussion with the class.

This large reading list in original materials excluded modern scholarship largely from Contemporary Civilization and almost entirely from Humanities. The staffs of these courses justified this lack in several ways. First, they asserted that students read the very best commentators on Plato or Sophocles: Aristotle and Aristophanes, to say nothing of Milton, Montaigne, and Spinoza. The books are connected, not only as members of a species, in Arthur Danto's sense, but as participants in a continuing enterprise, attacking, defending, imitating, parodying, and annotating their predecessors. The latest word of scholarship is not the last word, and must be added to the reading list only if it actually ranks with the masters of the past millennia. Second, and more importantly, these courses defined themselves as places to engage a text as directly as possible. As one group phrased it at the time:

> The course had traditionally avoided readings which might offer
> prefabricated formulations as a substitute for genuine intellectual
> intercourse with the book. The Columbia students long to be told,
> "What does Plato say?" And they have responded with shock,
> frustration, and genuine intellection to the traditional answer of [the
> course]: "read Plato."

A teacher enters class aware that certain readers have considered Molière's Misanthrope a tragic figure. Instead of informing the students of this fact, the effective teacher will direct the discussion to those passages in the play which provoked this response and, with a little luck, will find a student to take this position about the play. By then directing attention to other lines, a teacher can produce totally different formulations, so that the class does not so much learn what scholars have discovered as recapitulate their discovery.

A good Humanities or CC class requires a teacher able to see a text in an intricate context, and to control any part of it that the class discussion may turn to. In the process of developing staffs able to perform the first of these tasks and willing to perform the second, year after year, Columbia solved a series of administrative problems in ways that do much to explain the survival of general education at Columbia to this day, as well as its impact around the country. First, Columbia had no separate staff or budget for these courses. Every teacher belonged to one of the regular academic departments, and virtually all of them taught two courses in their department in addition to Humanities or CC.

The staffs of the Humanities and Contemporary Civilization courses had always consisted of five or ten senior professors with tenure, and a body of graduate students and junior staff. Until the 1950s these junior teachers largely bore the rank of instructor, and were full-time members of a department. There were never very many instructors at Columbia, and the general education courses constituted an introduction into their departments and the university world. After mastering the course and learning about the university, most of these instructors went on teaching for several years. Then some became professors at Columbia, while the majority, who left Columbia, are now teaching all over the country. Some of them have carried the spirit of innovation with them, like those who started the Great Books program at Chicago.

In the 1950s after finishing these two enormous courses, a student would continue his general education with Music Humanities, Art Humanities (one term each), and Contemporary Civilization B. Regardless of his specialty he would also have to study three years of a language and two of mathematics or a natural science. The science departments were never able to produce a common course like Humanities or CC, although they tried several times.

The Department of Art History, which includes a great diversity of specialties, solved the problem of a common course in a way that they described as follows:

> In its form and in its approach, Humanities FB is similar to Humanities A. Like it, Humanities FB deals with a limited number of topics in the visual arts that correspond in their place within the European tradition to the books in Humanities A. Examples are the architecture and sculpture of the Parthenon, or of Amiens Cathedral, the paintings of Raphael, Rembrandt, or Picasso, and the sculpture of Michelangelo. No attempt, however, is made to be exhaustive in any topic.

Like Humanities A, Humanities FB grows from the works themselves. Therefore, although the examples are generally presented in chronological order (and even this is not always true), it is not a history of art. No attempt whatever is made to trace the origins or development of the topics selected, or to sketch in even the briefest manner the art of the centuries that intervene between one topic and the next. However, since the problems faced by Bernini in sculpture were themselves conditioned by the ideas and ideals of his day, the students must try to recognize the imprint of these ideals in the works themselves. For this purpose, wherever possible, pertinent parallels are drawn to the work in Humanities A or Contemporary Civilization or any other sources of information the students are likely to have. Examples might be certain similarities in design between Greek drama and Greek architecture and sculpture; the occasional scatological details of Rabelais or Breughel; the character and concept of a gentleman of Baldassare Castiglione.

Nor is Humanities FB a philosophy of art in the sense that it tries to develop a consistent and complete body of aesthetic dogma. Some aesthetic concepts constantly recur in the course but essentially as they form part of the works themselves, not as abstract ideas.

The course is based on two premises. The first is, in the language of Ruskin, that "art is a noble and expressive language." If it is a language it must be intended to communicate something—presumably the ideals and interests of the artist and his age and place. It must, therefore, be capable of being read and understood if examined thoughtfully. In order to reach such understanding, the second premise is essential: that the students, and for that matter literate people of any age, have become so accustomed to receiving information only through the printed or spoken word that they never really look at anything, despite the Chinese proverb that one picture is worth a thousand words. They use their eyes only to recognize where they are and whom they see, without reflecting why the forms they see are arranged in a certain manner, or even why those particular forms were chosen in the first place. . . . Toward the end of the semester, the students are sent to examine selected original paintings or works of sculpture at the Metropolitan Museum, the Frick Gallery, and the Museum of Modern Art. Reading is assigned, but its role is secondarily to serve as general background to the periods that produced the works of art to be considered. The general education courses at Columbia College have in common a complete reliance on documents and a corollary indifference to secondary material. The painting, statue, or building itself is the important thing. In fact it is essential that the students should discover the form and content of the works themselves, without having their ideas shaped beforehand by even the most penetrating written analysis.

The music department faced the same problem of illiteracy in a nonverbal art and handled it in a similar way. [see appendix 1]

After the sophomore year, except for the Colloquium which we have already described, general education at Columbia existed primarily at the postdoctoral level, in the University Seminars. A University Seminar is a group of ten to thirty people who meet once or twice a month to discuss a field or problem about which they have different kinds of expertise. The members include Columbia faculty members, faculty members from other institutions in New York and all over the country, but also experts from the worlds of politics, industry, entertainment, and so forth. No one receives course credit for participating in these seminars, and the pay for a speaker ranges upwards and downwards from a free dinner. At times some seminars have been able to pay travel expenses for speakers and members, at other times not. Membership is by invitation only, and vacancies in most seminars are rare. The number of seminars has increased from five in 1945 (on the State, the Renaissance, Rural Life, Religion and Culture, and The Problem of Peace) to more than sixty in 1975. The number has stabilized more for economic than for intellectual reasons, and the example of these seminars has stimulated many other groups to meet regularly for similar discussions. Many of these seminars issue minutes of their meetings to their members; many are strictly informal. Many books have emerged directly from seminar discussions, and dozens more have profited from seminar critiques of chapters that were read as papers there. About seventy of these seminars meet regularly; in a given year, a few will be dormant, and a few moribund, but the enterprise as a whole is flourishing. It continues general education for scholars after they have completed the official steps in their education. [See appendix 5]

In this way, rather than letting our education end when our training begins, the University Seminars shape the awarenesses of the teachers in a way that makes them particularly receptive to the broader implications of their subject matter.

10   In the 1970s Columbia began to adapt this system to deal with intellectual and administrative pressures

We have described the evolution of an educational system which matched the needs of the fifties. This system survives more or less intact, and the rest of this book will deal with its adaptation to the problems of the seventies as we have already described them. Certain of these adaptations are obvious. If many students have not learned to handle outrageous loads of homework, we can adjust the assignments to a level only a little higher than most of them feel they can manage. Such an adjustment has its costs, but it does not affect the basic nature of the enterprise. Another obvious lack in the program was any attention at all to non-European traditions. This lack was remedied in the 1950s by the courses in Oriental civilization which were built up by Wm. Theodore de Bary on the model of Humanities and CC. Oriental CC dealt with historical and political problems in Japan, China, India, and the Arab world, and Oriental Humanities read masterpieces from all those civilizations. (See appendixes 1, 2)

As the fifties progressed, problems arose which could not be solved by tinkering. Some of these were social: as Arthur Danto reminded our seminar,

> In the 1920s and 1930s, when general education came up, it wasn't just an abstract idea that somebody had, thinking it would be nice to have some. Rather, it was a response to a social demand of a highly significant sort that was internalized. And the form of response was the general education course of the sort that we were pretty familiar with here at Columbia and, to some degree, at the University of Chicago. That was fine; and I daresay you really did turn out a certain kind of citizens . . . equipped with attitudes towards life and towards their own practices and values. Again in the 1950s society needed . . . a lot of people equipped to do very special kinds of jobs . . . . And disciplinary education of that sort really did furnish society with lots of people of just the sort that society needed; that is to say, the educational structure defined, more or less, the mode of citizenship that was expected of people who went through that structure. [*Seminar Reports* I, iii, 7]

Certainly the background and the ambitions of an average suburban student today differ sharply from those of the World War II
veterans of a generation ago and the children of immigrants of two
generations ago. And certainly the changes in our cultural and
intellectual world have affected the position of general education at
every university in the country. The patterns at various universities
lead us to the conclusion Daniel Bell reached in his discussion with
our seminar:

> There were as there are in such cases, intellectual elements; but the
> primary reasons were fundamentally institutional. These were: the rise
> of professionalism, the expansion of the graduate schools, the emphasis
> on disciplines;. . . the strengths of the departments against the college,
> . . . and the emphasis on research, all of which pulled people away from
> general education and into these other areas. [Seminar Reports I, iii, 4]

These trends operated everywhere, but the impact on general education varied. At Columbia, the system has retained its vigor and
its capacity for exploiting the discontent of an actively engaged
teaching company. At Harvard the administration is actively fostering such discontent with the current system. As the Dean of the
Faculty of Arts and Science, Henry Rosovsky, put it:

> The elements that make up Harvard College are often in conflict with
> one another. Frequently these conflicts are perceived as being between
> general education and the departments, between the academic role of the
> college and the non-academic activities of the college students, between
> the various disciplines, and between the college and the graduate school
> as these impinge upon each other and compete for diminishing financial
> resources. Faculty hiring and promotion policy, which ideally seeks a
> balance of abilities, in practice favors research over teaching; the lack of
> institutional rewards for teaching in general, and lower level instruction
> in particular, inevitably work to the disadvantage of undergraduates,
> especially in their first two years. . . .
> In recent years, adaptations of the curriculum at Harvard have tended
> to multiply options and reduce requirements. At present we seem to
> have reached an uneasy comprise between extremes, allowing enough
> freedom to make the contraints seem arbitrary, while constraining
> choices just enough to require justification of the limits placed on them.
> The drift towards a (qualified) free elective system, reflecting in large
> part the hegemony of the departments, has gradually eroded the

legitimacy of general education and other requirements . . . . Similarly, the variety of the *General Education* offerings—and in some cases their resemblance to departmental courses—make this requirement difficult to undertand *per se*. [*A Letter to the Faculty on Undergraduate Education*, October 1974]

At Chicago, where the seed sown at Columbia flourished the most flamboyantly, Leonard Meyer has described the scene as follows:

It is mostly gone now. Only a few vestiges remain. The question is: what happened? The reasons for the demise of the Hutchins College are many and complex; I will touch upon only a few. . . .

Though the Chicago situation was in some ways "special," what happened there was symptomatic of much broader, more fundamental changes which were taking place throughout higher education in the United States. The trend toward specialization and the concomitant process of disciplinary subdivision begun late in the nineteenth century accelerated markedly during the 1940s and '50s. With this was coupled a rapid growth in collegiate education after World War II. There was an enormous demand for teachers and, because of the accreditation standards, for those with the Ph. D. Increasingly, graduate departments and schools came to dominate universities, determining not only their own programs but (through their entrance requirements) the undergraduate curriculum as well. The undergraduate program at Chicago, for instance, was—and is—affected by the graduate entrance requirements at Columbia, Harvard, and Berkeley (and, of course, at Chicago as well).

As the number of applicants to graduate schools increased and as emphasis upon specialization grew, entrance requirements increased. Where before the War the calculus might have been included as part of a graduate program in biology, it soon became a prerequisite for admission to a graduate department. While before the War, graduate English departments often required nothing more specific than a B.A. from a reputable institution, they began to demand a series of survey courses in English literature on the undergraduate level for entrance. The colleges that sought to get their students into good graduate departments had to comply, or they would not have gotten students. They complied by taking courses away from the area of general education. Not only this, but it seems probable that the courses in the area of the major have become less liberal in character.

The trend toward specialization and the increased emphasis upon graduate education had a marked effect upon the staffing of general education courses. As the graduate schools came to dominate universities, they began to control the hiring and promotion process. Junior faculty soon recognized that advancement depended upon publication and the teaching of specialized courses. They became less interested in teaching general education courses. Moreover, their own training as specialists made many young faculty unwilling—embarrassed—to teach in fields even a little removed from their own. Economists wanted to teach only economics, and would not consider an introductory sociology course; Renaissance art historians wanted to teach only Renaissance Art History. To do otherwise was felt to be somehow dishonest. (What they failed, of course, to realize is that all education is a movement from greater error to less. They were confident that they had been taught the *Truth,* and that was what they intended to teach.) [*Seminar Reports* I, viii, 7]

At Columbia, the pressures have been the same. The social scientists, especially, mimicked the natural scientists in their mathematization, subdivision of fields, and disregard for outsiders. In describing the abolition of the second year of Contemporary Civilization, Peter Gay uses language exactly like that which described the Chicago scene:

> Then with the early 1960s things began to change. We became more professional, which is to say, more self-centered. The senior faculty dropped away; most of the junior faculty wished that it, too, could drop away. Word got around that promotion, let alone tenure, depended on performance in departmental courses, and above all in publication, both of them impeded by concentration on general education. Generalists became rare; they were, by and large, potential failures or real suckers. Prestige attached, not to getting into general education, but to getting out of it. The course that was pushed over in 1968-69 was already a push-over. [*Seminar Reports* I, v, 8]

And yet, except for the dropping of this course, and of one year of the science requirement, Columbia's system of requirements and general courses remains intact. Humanities and CC have no staff of their own, and must go begging among chairmen of departments every year. But they are often begging among professors and chairmen who themselves learned to teach in the course. Humanities has always had between five and ten senior professors among its thirty-odd teachers, and at present the number is at the top of the range. These older professors do not necessarily teach any better than those half their age, but their accumulated experience in the course is available, formally and informally, to the younger staff. The greatest pressure upon these courses from the changed times affects the junior staff, and it has come not from student pressures, as at Chicago, not from faculty pressures, as at Harvard, but from administrative pressures which have not been strong enough to destroy the integrity of these staffs. The Columbia administration recognizes that graduate students need money and need teaching experience. By replacing each old full-time instructorship with several part-time preceptorships designed to last as briefly as possible, the administration can spread these benefits over more graduate students. It takes, however, a year or two to turn most graduate students into teachers in a course as intricate as Humanities or CC. The process moves fastest when graduate students are in contact, not only with their seniors, but with colleagues who were making the same mistakes a year or two earlier. Rapid turnover deprives the newest teacher of contact with these trained younger colleagues and forces those trained younger colleagues to seek jobs elsewhere for which they must prepare all over again.

The administrative onslaught at Columbia, however, was intended not to destroy but to exploit general education, and faculty and student support for general education prevented its being sacrificed to the economic needs of graduate students. However, the malaise which Columbia shared with the rest of the educational world as a whole revived the curricular self-consciousness of the Columbia community.

⫸ PLANS AND PROJECTS ⫷

4

11

We have set up a general education seminar and also seminars in which the professional schools work closely with the departments of arts and sciences

In the late 1960s Columbia and the Carnegie Corporation had set up the smallest in the long series of committees that had reexamined general education over the years. The committee consisted of Professor Daniel Bell. Bell's book, *The Reforming of General Education,* stimulated long and serious discussion in the Columbia faculty. Among Bell's proposals, the idea of a "third tier" appealed most to the Columbia faculty. Bell believed that general education could no longer stop with the first year or two of undergraduate study. He proposed an array of courses at the upper-class level to draw students back into broad contact with the intellectual world during their concentration on their major specialty. The faculty saw great value in such a requirement, but realized that it would take a number of years to generate the courses to satisfy it. The discussions and plans that followed the appearance of Bell's book were interrupted by the crises of 1968-72, but in more recent years the Committee on General Education has returned to many of these ideas and has been working to advance general education, not only on the undergraduate level, but also on the graduate level and in the professional schools. Any such effort to introduce widespread reform in a university needs a broad forum to pool the contributions of specialists in all areas of teaching, administration, and student life, and also to make available to all of these constituencies an understanding of the thinking that is going on and of the process by which new ideas emerge.

Recognizing the need for such a forum, the Carnegie Corporation made available to Columbia the funds to establish the Thursday Seminars whose discussions form the backbone of this book. In the autumn of 1973 these seminars opened a series of discussions of the nature, goals, and techniques of general education. A cross section of students, faculty, and administrators from a dozen schools within the university listened to presentations by scholars and educators from Columbia and from major institutions all over the country. (See appendix 4 for list of topics and speakers.)

In the second year, the talks and the discussions that followed them explored examples of particular courses and programs which had proved or might prove effective in general education. Professors from Columbia who planned to give such courses offered sample lectures and overall discussions of the course for the criticism and suggestions of the assembled group. In most cases the audience consisted of a substantial number of students and faculty with a particular interest in the speaker's topic, plus a community of "regulars" who had built up a continuing sense of membership in the general education seminars.

In the third year the meetings were devoted to two topics: in the first semester to the professions and professionalism, and in the second semester to the teaching of science to both scientists and nonscientists.

In the fourth year most of the lectures are devoted to a discussion of liberalism and liberal education.

The talks appeared for the first two years as inserts in the Columbia newspaper, *The Spectator.* More recently they have appeared in a series of pamphlets called *Seminar Reports,* the same title they had in *Spectator,* but now printed in their own format. *Seminar Reports* now has several hundred readers off campus.

As a second way to stimulate interest in an awareness of general education, the committee has published a brochure each year listing several dozen courses and seminars that serve some of the purposes to which Daniel Bell had directed attention. Some of the courses in this brochure are designed to remedy the isolation of the professional schools which we have already discussed above. To overcome the isolation, the Committee on General Education turned to the Rockefeller Foundation, which has helped them to set up a series of seminars whose staff and students come from the professional schools and the arts and sciences faculties, especially in the humanities. This experiment has appealed to the desires of faculty members and administrators in both professional schools and the faculties of arts and sciences.

In each of these seminars, a professor from arts and sciences works with a professor from a professional school on a series of case studies centered on a problem of current and wide concern. Students come from several branches of the university. All of these seminars are designed to produce materials whose publication will be of use either to professionals in the field or to teachers anxious to give similar courses.

The seminar based in the School of Journalism was not conventionally academic. Michael Wood of the English Department and Fred Friendly of the Graduate School of Journalism led a multidisciplinary study of a five-year period in recent American history, 1949-54. Fifteen students eventually enrolled in the course. They were selected from approximately fifty applicants. The students finally admitted were chosen both for their ability and for the varieties of disciplinary experience they might bring to the study of those five years. In the end, students came from the Graduate School of Business, Columbia College, the School of the Arts, Teachers College, the Graduate School of Journalism, Barnard College, the School of General Studies, and the Graduate School of Arts and Sciences, majoring in journalism, history, political science, English, comparative literature, psychology, film, education, and marketing. (Students ranged in age from nineteen to thirty-four.)

Professors Wood and Friendly conceived the course as an opportunity to study the reflections of American public life in the media and the arts. Professor Friendly brought his experience in broadcasting to bear on this general area, and Michael Wood examined the various "texts" from the standpoint of a literary critic. During the semester the seminar looked closely at works of cinema, television, radio, literature, the press, and the theater.

They chose the years 1949-54 because of the important events taking place. As Professor Wood wrote in an early course description, these were the years of the Hiss case, Eisenhower's landslide election, McCarthy's anticommunist crusade, the Oppenheimer case, the birth of the civil rights movement, blacklisting, and the cold war. The course was organized around a group of "texts" which related closely to the historical events. In discussing the McCarthy era, for example, the class saw Edward R. Murrow's interviews with J. Robert Oppenheimer, Murrow's program on McCarthy, and read extensively in historical materials. Even more importantly, however, several of the central figures of this period visited the seminar and took part in spirited exchange. Alger Hiss and Roy Cohn discussed their roles in the anticommunist witch hunts. Ralph Ellison talked about his work and the early days of the civil rights movement. John Houseman discussed the systematic blacklisting of people in the entertainment fields.

During special sessions of the seminar—it ended up meeting approximately six hours per week and sometimes more—students viewed important films of the early 1950s. Such films as *Bad Day at Black Rock, Viva Zapata, A Place in the Sun, Pinky, The Black-board Jungle, Intruder in the Dust, Iron Curtain, The Bad and the Beautiful* were studied for the aesthetic questions they raised and for their connection with historical events.

The course generated much excitement and produced some interesting writing. The course also raised questions about interdisciplinary efforts and multi-teacher undertakings. One point of conflict emerged during the semester, was never resolved, and perhaps should not be resolved. The students working in conventional academic disciplines, such as history or political science, were often criticized by the journalists for being too "intellectual." The journalists wanted to see the people involved in the historical events—they were happiest when actually confronting Alger Hiss or Roy Cohn. The historians wanted to talk about the historical approach, look at the materials already written on the period and, in short, function as historians.

In the course description, Professors Wood and Friendly wrote that the seminar "should provide a portrait of a period; some understanding of the nature of history, especially the less formal kinds of history; and considerable communication across the barriers of separate disciplines." Whatever else the course has done, it has attained these goals.

A second seminar, based in the School of International Affairs, brought together a philosopher, Arthur Danto, and a historian of India, Ainslie Embree, who is also Associate Dean of the School of International Affairs. Their aim was to examine some of the major systems of Oriental thought, analyzing the moral attitudes they prescribe and the factual beliefs they presuppose. Professors Danto and Embree attempted to explore these systems, not merely for their intrinsic interest, but as definitions of the relationships between moral language and the language used to describe the world. The course pursued other goals: finding some basis for cross-cultural criticism; determining the extent to which values may be borrowed from one system by another. Arthur Danto's *Mysticism and Morality* served as a text for initiating discussion, but the basic sources were readings in translation from the Oriental traditions and students were forced to reevaluate their own beliefs and moral attitudes in light of those works.

Students were required to participate in discussion and were asked to write papers giving their reactions to one of the works read in the course. In some cases, students were unable to break away from summarizing the research done by others. Most student work demonstrated a willingness to examine both the student's own presuppositions and those of the great thinkers of the Oriental tradition.

Professors Danto and Embree worked out a complex instructional arrangement for the course. They functioned as team teachers, assisted by Robin Martin, a graduate student of Chinese government. During the semester, other scholars participated, presenting papers for class discussion. Speakers included:

Professor Robert McDermott, Department of Philosophy, Baruch College. "The Moral Ideas of the Bhagavad-Gita."

Professor Wayne Proudfoot, Department of Religion, Columbia. "Religion and Morality: Is Morality Specific to a Culture?"

Professor Anthone Cua, Department of Philosophy, Catholic University. "Confucian Attitudes and Facual Beliefs."

Professor Chung-ying Cheng, Department of Philosophy, University of Hawaii. "Harmony and Conflict in Chinese Philosophy."

Professor Wm. Theodore de Bary, Vice-President for Academic Affairs, Columbia. "Confucianism."

Our third professional school seminar was based in the College of Physicians and Surgeons. Officially known as the "Health Sciences General Education Seminar on Ethics and Values in Health Care," the seminar attracted approximately forty students and faculty from both the Morningside Heights campus and the medical school. The seminar was divided into four task forces, listed below, which considered topics selected by a seminar steering committee:

1. Issues in Reproduction
2. Behavior Modification and Control
3. Allocation of Health Care Resources
4. Death and Survival

The task forces met weekly to discuss papers, consider case histories, work out research problems, and met together once a month in a session with a major speaker, open to the public. On occasion, outside speakers attended the seminars; for example, Colin Murray Parkes, the British thanatologist, visited the seminar on survival and dying. Students came from philosophy, religion, English, history, public health, and medicine. As Professor Steven Marcus, the leader of the task force on behavior modification and control, has said: "No one was an expert in the areas we were studying. We were all amateurs, and we could therefore become students again." Indeed, one of the great benefits of the seminars is that normal distinctions between student and teacher have become blurred. Each participant feels that he or she is part of a team working on an important problem.

Some of the problems discussed this year include: professionalization of physicians; the doctor-patient relationship; the assumptions and values implicit in official hospital records; the formulation of behavioral models for human beings; the ethical and value questions in obstetrical and gynecological counseling; the establishment of hostels for the dying; historical attitudes toward death and dying; medical school curriculum, and a number of other questions.

In the spring of 1976, the School of Architecture set up a seminar on housing in New York. This seminar included students from the School of Architecture, Department of Urban Planning, the Law School, the Graduate Department of Sociology, one Barnard undergraduate, and one Columbia College undergraduate. The students work with five "tutors" who are experts in planning, financing, construction, administration, and sanitation. In addition to the urban planning leaders, Richard Plunz and Jacqueline Levitt, five visiting experts have addressed the seminar. In addition to the group work of the seminar, there have been five meetings with special speakers open to the public. (See appendix 4.)

As a part of this seminar, the students of urban planning and architecture have been designing projects to correct the mistakes and solve the problems they have been studying together.

In 1977, we are offering a seminar in professional ethics for engineers. In this course Professor Stephen Unger plans to work in collaboration with an engineer, a lawyer, a journalist, and a philosopher on the topic of professional ethics in the narrow sense of the word, the ways a profession develops rules for its members' behavior, and enforces those rules, and protects professionals against harassment for observing those rules.

Like all the other seminars, Professor Unger's will tend to use the case system presenting particular episodes on which ample materials are available and bringing the resources of the various disciplines to bear in coming to an understanding of these episodes.

12

We are organizing teaching companies to restore coherence among the isolated parts of the university

After a decade in which students felt institutional, peer, and family pressure to specialize narrowly in established disciplines, careers today often call for broader and more versatile backgrounds. We have discussed the conflict between the purists in the established disciplines and those who hope to serve the broader social need: if a university abandons the traditional organization of its curriculum into disciplines and its teaching staff into departments, it is likely to lose the fruits of two centuries' division of labor; if it does not, it must devise educational instruments to keep students in touch with the historical, philosophical, sociological, ecological, and other implications of their work in their specialty. Failure to find such instruments can lead to a generation unfit to deal with the complexities of modern life. We are working to set up teaching companies to put at the disposal of departmental majors the resources of several departments in a given area of study.

Besides using Humanities, CC, and the University Seminars as instruments to broaden the education of its freshmen and its postdoctoral staff, Columbia has pioneered one other kind of general education of a very specialized kind. In response to national needs in the 1940s, it set up regional institutes in such areas as the Soviet Union, East Asia, Western Europe, and the Middle East. Students enrolled in one of these institutes earn certificates indicating that they have taken courses in a number of departments dealing with a geographical region. All courses and all faculty members in these institutes belong to existing departments.

Columbia was one of the first universities in the 1940s to mix education with training by blurring the boundaries between disciplines and professions. For example, the Russian Institute was founded by a professor in the Law School, an economist, a historian, a professor of literature, and a professor of international relations. Students in the institute planned careers in both government and scholarship, and took courses in economics, government, history, international affairs, and literature at the same time that they were taking an M.A. in one of those fields. The program served its national purpose, and our first substantial generation of Russian experts emerged from such institutes all over the country. Columbia has similar institutes now to study other geographical areas. As general education, these area studies offered an important lesson: experts in one academic discipline can and should do advanced work in another discipline at points where the two impinge. The good area studies programs proved that students can profit from advanced studies in a related field, if they are able to exploit the relationship to their own field in place of the usual prerequisites. Graduate students in Russian literature can learn a great deal from a course in Soviet economics without any prior study of economics. Their incapacities will often be more in basic data or terminology, which are easily acquired, than in systematic ways of proceeding, which good lecturers often have to reestablish for their majors in such courses anyway.

Using the Humanities and CC programs, the University Seminars and the regional institutes as models, we are developing a new kind of teaching company, one that can deal at the graduate and advanced undergraduate level with areas of study that are defined intellectually or historically rather than geographically. Many such areas are not the responsibility of any single department, but constitute a major center of interest for several dozen faculty members. Over the past two years we have been talking with teachers involved in Renaissance studies, medieval studies, applied psychoanalysis, drama and theater, religion and culture, aesthetics and the theory of criticism. Most years, Columbia offers from one to four dozen courses in each of these areas of study. Until we began to work with our colleagues, many of them were so isolated that they had not met one another, and none of them knew the full scope of Columbia's existing program in their area. In fact, Columbia did not have a program in these areas so much as a collection of courses and occasional student interdepartmental majors.

In each of these areas we have found scholars who are willing to take the lead in turning such groups into working organizations. Their first step is to compile a complete list of all courses given in the area over a two-to-three-year period. The second step, taken in close cooperation with the teaching company and with the departments in which these courses are given, is the rationalization of that list. In some cases this rationalization forces the area to define the basic body of information necessary for entering students. An introductory course may be necessary to provide students with the proper preparation for existing courses. In other cases students who have already taken several courses in an area may need a "cap" course to bring together the skills and awarenesses acquired in various departments. During this rationalization process, the faculty members also educate each other.

In many areas the paracurricular work of the teaching company is as important as the actual rationalization of courses. Certain groups are eager to have regular meetings to hear presentations by faculty and students. As the teaching companies become more coherent, we predict that all of them will move toward this kind of interdepartmental contact. In most of these areas a mimeographed newsletter to inform faculty and students about public events, lectures, and news of the area can be of great value not only to the Columbia community but to specialists in neighboring institutions. If the area of study develops the kind of coherence which the geographical institutes have achieved at Columbia, such a newsletter could also be used to call the attention of faculty and students to important articles in obscure journals and in general to keep them alert to the developments in their field. Such an unpretentious collaborative venture needs the energies of a student research assistant and the help of a secretary on a part-time basis, but most of all its success depends upon the coherence of the teaching company.

As these teaching companies develop an identity, each develops its own momentum. Out of their own resources the teaching companies will be able to establish "outreach courses" taught as a series of lectures with different members taking turns. This contact with the community need not be formalized as a course. The teaching company may arrange special lectures in collaboration with other parts of the university or organize "Festivals," conferences lasting a day or more to draw the attention of the public and the scholarly world to a major figure, problem, or subject in the area. To illustrate the possibilities for such teaching companies, we present a description by our colleagues of work being done in two areas of study, one defined historically—Medieval Studies—and one defined conceptually and methodologically, still problematical in its final organization—Scientific Areas.

MEDIEVAL STUDIES

The English and the history departments at Columbia both have a substantial number of major medievalists on their staffs, but medieval materials play a major part in over 75 courses each year which are scattered over an array of departments, including German, French, Italian, religion, music, philosophy, Greek and Latin, Slavic, art history, and Near and Middle-Eastern languages.

In addition to the resources of these departments, and to the libraries and other collections, we have in our immediate neighborhood the Union Theological Seminary and the Jewish Theological Seminary. The remarkable medieval library at Jewish Theological Seminary has made it a major center for the study of Jewish thought in that period, while Union now has the services of some of the foremost historians of medieval theology and church history. The Cathedral of St. John the Divine, also one block from the university, has become a vital center for the New York revival of medieval music, offering an ideal setting for performances by the New York Cornet and Sackbut Ensemble, the New York Concert of Viols, the Ensemble for Early Music, and other successors to the Noah Greenberg Pro Musica Antiqua. Students and faculty have at their disposal the collections of the Brooklyn Museum, the Metropolitan Museum and the Cloisters, the New York Public Library, and the rich manuscript holdings of the Morgan Library.

To use these resources better at the curricular level, our teaching company plans to collate the entire medieval offering, undergraduate and graduate, at the university and nearby institutions (Union and Jewish Theological Seminaries), publicizing it to all departments, suggesting needed courses to faculty members who might give them, and lobbying on behalf of departments that would like to make appointments to improve such coverage.

Their other major responsibility will be advising undergraduate and graduate students of medieval courses available throughout the university, helping them plan appropriate programs to use these resources, and perhaps offering guidance in job-seeking and other matters relating to postgraduate and postdoctoral advancement (conferences, journals, competitions, and so forth).

Each term, this group would like to prepare a listing of all medieval courses offered in university and neighboring institutions, asking faculty members to avoid time conflicts, and to list their courses as (a) introductory, (b) intended primarily for majors, or (c) "cap" courses for advanced majors from more than one discipline. This listing should be available at the beginning of the term to which it applies, to aid students at registration.

To encourage these "cap" courses, faculty members wishing to teach such courses alone or in teams should receive help with clerical work, publicity, and, in certain cases, released time. As such courses appear, a rational rotational sequence can be arranged.

The teaching company should organize a guidance committee of two or three faculty members who will be identified to the student body as willing to discuss work in medieval studies at the undergraduate or graduate level. These would not be official representatives of any department or program, but faculty who would have all available material about medieval courses and programs, and would offer advice to students who seek them out.

At the paracurricular level, the teaching company plans to set up events—conferences, speakers, colloquia—of an interdisciplinary as well as disciplinary nature, creating initiatives to supplement the official offerings on a noncredit basis. Paracurricular experiments may, of course, ultimately receive official status as courses, if faculty and departments wish. The main task of this activity, however, is enrichment—the establishment of a medieval ambience that is adventurous, exciting, intellectually respectable but innovative, supportive of departmental offerings, yet able to go beyond them in brief, less-structured formats.

The group hopes to invite distinguished speakers and set up one-day or multi-day conferences on medieval subjects like the Piers Plowman Festival arranged in April 1976 by students and faculty in the Departments of English and Comparative Literature, History, Art History, Philosophy, and Music; Barnard College Medieval and Renaissance Studies Program; Casa Italiana; University Seminar in Medieval Studies; individual departments. The main beneficiaries of such events would be the university's students and faculty, though for some special occasions an event could be scheduled to which medievalists from the city or a wider community would be invited. Examples: (a) a conference on the Twelfth-Century Renaissance, with emphasis on intellectual and scholastic developments; (b) a series on court culture and its achievements in the Middle Ages; (c) colloquia on the place of women in theory and practice in medieval society; (d) a series on medieval towns and cities—urban problems and achievements (illustrated surveys of York, Chartres, Ravenna, and so forth).

The company of teachers also plans to establish a monthly colloquium at which a team of students and faculty from different departments explores the interdisciplinary dimensions of a project or problems on which they are working within their respective disciplines; presentations followed by discussion. All medieval students and faculty should be invited; they would set up the schedule a term in advance. These colloquia can bring students and faculty together around issues of shared intellectual interest, establish a forum for and expectation of interdisciplinary conversation, and perhaps foster eventual interdisciplinary courses where advanced students can pool their disciplinary knowledge in confronting large medieval issues.

SCIENTIFIC AREAS

In general, the areas of study that have already begun operation provide intellectual benefits that far outweigh administrative inconveniences. As these areas of study develop, they may provide an intellectual environment for many of the educational innovations which our departments have been unable to organize. The natural scientists, as we have noted, find it extremely difficult to work together in deciding on a body of scientific understanding which they would like all undergraduates to have. Rather than trying to work out an exact body of materials, or to agree on what the scientific approach is, we should perhaps set a group of scientists to work on a phenomenon central to an area of study. Gerald Feinberg has suggested that such an approach may be the best way to teach science to nonspecialists.

> In any case, my own feeling is that even in physics, one can teach a good deal without much use of mathematics, and indeed that it may be useful to do so, since many students tend to confuse the content of physics with its mathematical expression anyway; and I think we should do our best to disabuse them of this confusion.
>
> One uncommon approach to the teaching of science, which I think could prove useful in elementary courses, is to structure a course around a specific phenomenon, rather than by the subdisciplines of the field. This could be done either in a given field such as physics, or even across several sciences. For example, we could have all, or part, of a course on the conversion and use of energy, or on the weather, or on some aspects of nutrition. I think this is useful because it can give students an indication of the explanatory power of science in situations that will seem less abstract or contrived to them than the usual textbook cases often do.
>
> Another useful device in teaching is to indicate some of the unsolved problems and open questions in each field. This helps students realize the essential fact that scientific discovery is an ongoing activity, and perhaps helps justify the great importance that most academic scientists attach to their research work. [*Seminar Reports* I, iv, 2]

If for example the Victorian era should emerge as an area of study at some time, we would hope to induce geologists and biologists to work with the philosophers, economists, and historians in developing an adequate course on Darwinism. As we have already pointed out, areas of study can be defined methodologically as well as historically. One such area which is now emerging is that of science and society. An example of the kind of problem that might come up in such an area of study was provided by James Darnell at a Thursday Seminar in which he discussed the biological and social problems connected with the work now being done on the DNA that carries genetic information.

A technique has now been devised which permits a piece of DNA to be taken out of a common bacterium that inhabits the human gut and to introduce it into an enzyme, thereby producing a molecule which is part human and part bacterium. Now, that feat of chemical magic is good enough by itself, you might think, but it also is possible to get this recombinant molecule back inside the bacterial cell. And thus it becomes possible to grow essentially unlimited amounts of a particular region of DNA, taken from any organism you care to choose. The technology in this field is advancing so rapidly that it will almost certainly soon be possible for any single human gene to be purified and put into bacteria. Moreover, after some appropriate interval, it will almost certainly be true that these bacteria can be made to synthesize human products in large amounts.

Assuming that the science goes as easily as I think it will, and if things are kept under proper control, we can expect immense benefits. For example, if we could synthesize large quantities of human growth hormone and human insulin, it is clear that these products could be used by doctors to treat patients whose growth or health is impaired by insufficient production of these hormones.

What, then, is the reason for introducing anything except a joyous note when we talk about these new techniques in public? The problem that has arisen is that the easiest bacterium in which to conduct these studies in the laboratory is an organism which (in some related form) inhabits our gut. What we do not know is whether a bacterium containing a human gene—for example, one that makes growth hormones—might not also be a terribly noxious agent to let loose in the environment. Most of us, having grown about as much as we would like, wouldn't care to have a gutful of bacteria producing growth hormones. In fact, of course, it might not do any harm, might never be absorbed. Nevertheless, the fear that we might be creating monsters caused a group of concerned scientists to stop and think several years ago. It is this process of scientists trying to think out loud, and asking for help from the public, that I now want to review for you.

In the summer of 1973, Maxime Singer of Yale and Dieter Soule from NIH, who were cochairing the Nucleic Acid Gordon Conference, recommended to the conference members that the implications of the

new techniques for recombinant DNA molecules—which they
recognized to be potentially explosive—be given serious consideration.
A communiqué came out of that Gordon Conference, directed to the
National Academy of Science, where the NAS Director, Dr. Handler,
then appointed an advisory committee to report to him on the public
policy implications of experimental activity in this field. That group,
composed of ten active scientists, signed a letter asking all the other
scientists in the world voluntarily to defer working on experiments in
this area until a conference could be convened at which the safety of this
technique could be openly discussed and guidelines arrived at. Such a
conference was convened in February 1975, at Asilomar, California,
attended by 150 people from 52 countries. The Asilomar conference
produced a set of guidelines which, to the best of my knowledge, have
been honored by scientists throughout the world with no serious
breaches over the last two years—despite the fact that many are itching
to get on with their very interesting experiments.

The Asilomar guidelines have now been reviewed by a committee
appointed by the Director of NIH and charged with drawing up a
proposed set of standards to be followed by NIH in considering grant
applications for projects of this sort. The proposed guidelines drawn up
by the NIH advisory committee, on which I have served, were similar to
those arrived at by the Asilomar scientists. They are now undergoing
review by the Director of NIH, with final recommendations from
another committee which has wider public representation than the
earlier group.

In the final analysis, I believe this is the way to make scientific policy,
for NIH, after all, supports 80 percent of the medical research in this
country. The people who have responsibility for the disbursement of
funds that support the science ought to decide what can, and what
cannot, be done with the public's money.

In summary, I believe that the very serious potential risks of these
techniques have been reviewed, the very real benefits have been
estimated, and some very sensible guidelines have been advocated. In
this instance, however, all this was done more or less haphazardly—
because a few concerned scientists had the perspicacity to see around
the corner and were willing to take the initiative in organizing
discussions of the potential problems they foresaw. The failure, if there
was one in this particular instance, lies in our not having had a standing
body ready to look into the potential benefits and risks of new biological
work. And I would like to suggest that if such an NIH advisory group is
now organized on a permanent basis, it should contain a richer

admixture of lay people than has been usual in the past. [*Seminar Reports* IV, iii, 23–25]

13 We are finding solutions for the problems implicit in such teaching companies

Courses dealing with new materials often go beyond the intellectual resources of any single teacher. For the first year or two they often demand the services of two or more professors. Columbia has used such pairs of teachers for many years in the College Colloquium and in various colloquia on science and philosophy. This kind of teaching presents problems which do not occur with companies of instructors who work together like the Humanities, CC staffs, and those in other areas of study, but who teach their classes separately. Some of these problems are economic—no university can afford to have two senior faculty members teaching a dozen undergraduates several hours a week in very many courses. But the expense is not merely economic. A team-taught course can consume more energy in planning and coordinating than two single courses, and is much harder to make rigorous.

The trauma involved in team teaching can be crucial in a program which cannot hope to find single experts in all the areas where courses are needed. Bernard Schoenberg gave our seminar a report on a study he had made in a course which tried to bring the expertise of sociologists and psychiatrists together. Because so many educators ignore this problem, we should like to cite Schoenberg at length:

> As we accumulated data on the interaction of the psychiatrist and sociologist in developing the interdisciplinary relationship, we were able to identify specific stages of collaboration, which we called:
> 1. Role Separation

2. Overestimation and Disappointment
3. Realistic Appraisal
4. Accommodation
5. Interchangeability of Roles
6. Theoretical Fusion

1. Role Separation

In the first stage, during the initiation of the programs each discipline responded according to its accustomed professional role. Although commitment to student education was verbalized and the need to establish a collaborative teaching relationship was recognized, it remained abstract and theoretical, while the sociologist and psychiatrist maintained fixed disciplinary boundaries. In retrospect, the strong disciplinary allegiance represented an effort to alleviate anxiety by sharply defining a disciplinary identity. The psychiatrist assumed the role of psychotherapist, and the sociologist assumed the role of observer of social interaction. Competition and anxiety, although manifest, were usually not verbalized.

2. Overestimation and Disappointment

As each discipline began to recognize the difficulties involved in achieving the program's goals, there was a tendency to turn to the other discipline for knowledge and technique. Overestimation of the other's possible contribution was accompanied by an oversimplification of the complex nature of the discipline. The unrealistic expectation was inevitably followed by disappointment. The tendency to retreat to a fixed disciplinary position persisted, and representatives of the one discipline were often overtly angry at members of the other. At this stage, some members of both disciplines found reasons to leave the teaching program and seek other teaching responsibilities which created minimal role strain.

3. Realistic Appraisal

As members of each discipline became aware of the contributions the other could make toward accomplishing the educational goals, there was a more realistic appreciation of the other. Confrontations were no longer motivated to indirectly establish the superiority of one discipline over the other, but rather to challenge stereotyped thinking and behavior. The disciplinary boundaries became less rigidly defined, and one discipline tended to assume a more sympathetic attitude toward the other in group discussions.

4. Accommodation

At this stage, progress toward role collaboration became apparent. Explanations tended to complement each other. Personal and disciplinary differences were easily recognized and verbalized, and mutually satisfying accommodations were realized.

5. Interchangeability of Roles

At this stage the disciplinary boundaries became highly permeable and roles were exchanged at an increased rate. Disciplinary interest focused on common meeting grounds, and roles were interchanged without apparent anxiety. The sociologist offered psychological interpretations, and the psychiatrist freely elaborated on certain aspects of social structure related to the patient. The frequency of stereotyped thinking and fragmented views of patients were markedly diminished. The strong identification of both the psychiatrist and the sociologist with the goals of the program was evident at this stage.

6. Theoretical Fusion

Later on in the process of collaboration, interest was expressed by both disciplines in integrating personality and social system theory. Some fruitful efforts on a theoretical level finally developed. [*Seminar Reports* II, v, 1-2]

Schoenberg's paper tends to confirm our own conclusions from observations of courses at Columbia's other campus—that team teaching of this sort is economically inefficient and hard to institute but, when successful, immensely valuable.

Team teaching educates professors as well as students. We have described the value of Humanities and CC for the education of teachers, especially as they were constituted in the 1950s, when younger faculty stayed with the course long enough to master it and teach their immediate successors. If the needs of the graduate school require a turnover of graduate-student teachers every year or two, we must find some more structured and intensive way to introduce them into the work of teaching. Drill or laboratory instruction for a senior teacher offers a student assistant either slack supervision or loss of freedom to improvise and grow; the student is often hesitant to bring his problems to a professor who will be deciding on his doctorate and perhaps his job; the undergraduates expect little of teaching assistants, and nobody but undergraduates ever sees them teach.

To improve the training of younger teachers and at the same time find teams to teach subjects too new or too complex for any available staff, it is possible to use teaching teams composed of a senior professor and a beginning teacher from another department. This pattern differs sharply from the traditional team of professor and graduate student, in which the junior member is in a distinctly subordinate position. In point of mere knowledge, a professor should have only a little to learn from someone much younger in his own department, but he will feel no embarrassment from learning from someone much younger in another department. This greater equality, however, will not produce the conflict of roles which Bernard Schoenberg described when two professors meet in the classroom. The difference in field will protect the status of the younger member of a well-matched team, forcing his senior to defer to him in the area of his expertise, and the difference in age will encourage the junior member to turn to his senior for help and example in the matter of pedagogy. He will be able to do this with greater security than in his own department, because his co-teacher has no departmental control over his destiny. We are working to establish a group of such teaching teams, educating undergraduates, graduate students, and professors at the same time.

To spread the awareness of this sort of teaching company, the Mellon Foundation and the Kenen Foundation are helping Columbia to set up a company of senior and junior scholars to be known as the Society of Fellows in the Humanities.

The existence of a company of students and distinguished faculty working together in this way should provide the long-needed competition with such departmental criteria for advancement as scholarly mastery of a narrowly defined field. Another set of rewards will exist for pedagogical promise and for interest in a related field. If either of these ideals excluded the other, the competition would impoverish our universities. Because education needs both, this little group will not only learn to teach but will lead many others to see that they need not choose between being scholars and being teachers who can see beyond the boundaries of discipline narrowly defined. We expect this company of older and younger teachers to be the kind of setting from which ideas and people may come to bring us to terms with our cultural crisis.

14 Other universities can profit from some of our ideas and some of our mistakes

The problems that we described have led Columbia to the kind of self-examination that it has undertaken once or twice in each decade for a century. In this examination the Carnegie Corporation has enabled us to open the discussions to the widest possible audience in our Thursday Seminars, and we have been able to work with members of every constituency in the university. The seminars have not only generated most of the ideas which have worked, but also produced several valuable criticisms. Peter Gay, for example, challenged the very idea of interdisciplinary study:

> Perhaps the best measure of our bad conscience about the decay of general education and the disappearance of the Renaissance ideal is the facile, anxious, ritualistic use of the word interdisciplinary. I do not think I am exaggerating when I say that this word has immense magical power with foundations and with the National Endowment for the Humanities—which is to say with those who have power over us. Any proposal that can conceivably be dressed up as interdisciplinary will be so dressed up. The fakery involved might be dismissed as harmless, as the conventional phrase that an encounter with a potential donor exacts. There is much to be said about the corrosive cynicism that such social graces entail. But cynicism is the least of the dangers that the fetish of the interdisciplinary poses. Far more dangerous is the situation that arises when we come to believe in what we say. [*Seminar Reports* I, v, 8]

We cannot dispute either of Peter Gay's assumptions, that fads get tawdry and that our existing disciplines are precious. As Professor Sidney Morgenbesser expressed it more tersely, "Who needs a course in torts and concerti?" But our work in interdisciplinary education at Columbia has outlasted all sorts of fads in the past century, and has continued to develop in response to real intellectual and social needs.

We are anxious not to threaten the existing disciplines and we realize, as we have already said, that any outside activity costs

professors and students time and energy which their chief disciplines desperately need. We see general education as a complement
to traditional scholarly disciplines. Columbia has never tried to
establish general education as a separate department or as a complete curriculum. We have finite goals; perhaps our students owe
their own humanity an intellectual tithe. And perhaps the university should organize its energies so that students at all levels can
give a portion of their thought and work to the following kinds of
courses:

1. Courses which heighten their self-consciousness of their own
field. This awareness may be historical, as in the history of physics; or theoretical, as in the philosophy of biology, the theory of
literature, historiography, or aesthetics. Sometimes the awareness
would be of other sorts, as in the sociology of the medical
profession.

2. Courses which make explicit the links between fields which
we always think of as somehow adjacent. Some of these areas have
already become fields in themselves, like comparative literature,
astrophysics, or biochemistry. But many remain to be incorporated
in areas of study which have not yet been established, and perhaps
never ought to become a student's specialty.

3. Courses which make available to one field the techniques of
another apparently remote from it, as in our courses in psychohis-
tory, or the semiotics of structures. Such courses can be intellectually risky, but the presence of trained students from both fields
makes them less so.

We began this study with a list of problems, some generated in
our educational system, and some impinging upon it from outside.
We have offered a collection of solutions to these problems, some
tried and proven over the years in Columbia College, and others
still in the experimental stage. Few of these solutions could be
adopted by other universities exactly as they have been conceived
and organized at Columbia, but we are certain that almost any
university can profit from some of our ideas and some of our
mistakes.

⇛ APPENDIXES ⇚

We have not written a how-to-do-it book, but the details of our work may prove useful to schools which might like to adapt certain elements of our curriculum to their needs. Columbia reading lists are constantly in flux, adjusting to the availability of editions, the interests of students and faculty, and also to the occasional reexaminations of our educational undertaking. For the various general education courses, we have included different kinds of information, depending upon the probable needs of our readers. We have also included information about two Columbia activities which are not courses but which offer general education to scholars and to the general public: the University Seminars and the Festivals. The appendixes are as follows:

1. Humanities
2. Contemporary Civilization
3. Seminar Reports
4. Professional School Seminars
5. The University Seminars
6. Festivals

⇒⇒ Humanities ⇐⇐

HUMANITIES A: COMPOSITE READING LIST

On page 54 we have given a typical reading list for Humanities A. Since 1937, the following readings have always appeared on the lists: *The Iliad, The Oresteia, Oedipus the King, The Peloponnesian War, The Republic, The Poetics, The Aeneid, The Confessions, The Inferno, Gargantua and Pantagruel,* Montaigne's *Essays, King Lear, Don Quixote.* The following list contains all the readings assigned between 1937 and 1969, when a final month of the course was turned over to books selected by the individual classes. In practice these selections have usually come from the same list.

Over the years the teachers have selected a series of translations and editions, usually deferring to the experts among their members on a given author, but considering the pedagogical appropriateness, the cost of the book, as well as scholarly accuracy and literary grace. In recent years, for example, we have used the Richmond Lattimore and the Robert Fitzgerald translations for Homer, tending most often to the Lattimore *Iliad* and the Fitzgerald *Odyssey.* Our students respond best to the Chicago series of translations of the Greek drama; and for the kind of reading this course demands, which is more literary than archeological, the King James Bible seems to work best.

In many cases works were not read in their entirety, others were optional.

Homer: *Iliad; Odyssey*
Aeschylus: *Oresteia; Prometheus Bound*
Herodotus: *The Persian Wars*
Sophocles: *Oedipus the King; Antigone; Oedipus at Colonus; Electra; Philoctetes; Ajax*
Euripides: *Electra; Iphigenia in Tauris; Medea; Trojan Women; Hippolytus; Bacchae; Alcestis; Heracles; Orestes*
Thucydides: *The Peloponnesian War*

Aristophanes: *Frogs; Clouds; Birds; Thesmophoriazusae; Peace; Lysistrata*

Plato: *Apology; Symposium; Timaeus; Euthyphro; Phaedrus; Meno; Protagoras; Phaedo; Gorgias; Ion; Crito; Republic*

Aristotle: *Poetics; Ethics; Psychology; Metaphysics; Statecraft; Metaphysics*

Lucretius: *The Nature of the Universe*

Lucian: *Satirical Sketches*

Marcus Aurelius: *Meditations*

Virgil: *Aeneid*

Tacitus: *Annals; Germany*

Bible: Job; Genesis; Amos; Ecclesiastes; Exodus; Isaiah; Hosea; Matthew; John; 1 Corinthians; Revelation; Romans; Proverbs; Song of Solomon

Apuleius: *The Golden Ass*

St. Augustine: *Confessions*

Dante: *Inferno; Purgatorio; Paradiso; Divine Comedy*

Machiavelli: *The Prince*

Rabelais: *Gargantua and Pantagruel,* 1 and 2 or 3

Wolfram: *Parzival*

Montaigne: *Essays; Raymond Sebond*

Shakespeare: *Henry IV, part 1; Henry IV, part 2; Twelfth Night; Hamlet; King Lear; As You Like It; Macbeth; The Tempest; Much Ado About Nothing; Measure for Measure; Troilus and Cressida; Antony and Cleopatra*

Cervantes: *Don Quixote*

Milton: *Paradise Lost; Samson Agonistes* and poems

Spinoza: *Ethics*

Descartes: *Meditations*

Molière: *Tartuffe; The Misanthrope; The Physician in Spite of Himself; The School for Wives; The Bourgeois Gentleman; The Would-Be Invalid; The Precious Damsels*

Swift: *Gulliver's Travels*

Fielding: *Tom Jones*

Hume: *Dialogues Concerning Natural Religion*

COLLOQUIUM

We have discussed the Colloquium on page 49. As a course for carefully selected juniors and seniors, it is the opposite of the required freshman Humanities A. In recent years, the reading list has been selected in conference between the students and the two professors for each semester, but it has not departed radically from the older sample list below, which is designed carefully to overlap as little as possible with the Humanities A reading list of two or three years earlier.

Colloquium 1

Homer: *Odyssey*

Hesiod: *Works and Days*

Homeric Hymns: *To Demeter; To Hermes*

Pindar: 1st Olympian Ode; 4th Pythian Ode

Aeschylus: *Suppliants; Seven against Thebes; Oresteia; Prometheus Bound*

Sophocles: *Ajax; Electra; Philoctetes; Oedipus at Colonus*

Euripides: *Electra; Alcestis; Hippolytus; Bacchae*

Aristophanes: *Lysistrata; Thesmophoriazusae; Peace; The Birds*

Thucydides: *The Peloponnesian War*

Plato: *Phaedrus; Parmenides; Timaeus;* 7th Letter

Virgil: *Eclogues; Georgics*

Longus: *Daphnis and Chloe*

Horace: *Satires*

Juvenal: *Satires*

Lucian: *The True History; Dialogues of the Gods; Dialogues of the Dead; Dialogues of the Courtesans; Philosophies for Sale*

Ovid: *Metamorphoses; Art of Love*

Seneca: *Thyestes; Phaedra*

Plautus: *Amphitryon; Rudens*

Terence: *Adelphi*

Tacitus: *Annals, 1–6; Germania*

Plutarch: *Isis and Osiris; Lives* (selections)

COLLOQUIUM 2

Plato: *Ion; Republic* books 3, 10

Aristotle: *Rhetoric, 3; Poetics*

Longinus: *On the Sublime*

Apuleius: *The Golden Ass*

Petronius: *Satyricon*

Genesis; Ecclesiastes; Psalms 1, 8, 19, 23, 29, 51, 90, 91, 104, 121, 128, 137, 139, 148, 150

Corinthians; Romans; Revelation

St. Augustine: *The City of God,* books 1, 5, 8, 11, 19

The Letters of Abelard and Heloise

The Romance of Tristan and Iseult; Aucassin and Nicolette

Dante: *The Divine Comedy*

Boccaccio: *Decameron,* 1:1; 2:9; 3:9; 4:1,5; 6:10; 7:7,9; 8:1,6; 10:5,10

Villon: *The Great Testament; The Little Testament; Ballads*

Chaucer: *Troilus and Criseyde*

Machiavelli: *Discourses; Mandragola*

Rabelais: Book 3

Castiglione: *The Courtier,* books 1, 4

Marlowe: *Doctor Faustus, Tamburlaine*

Webster: *The Duchess of Malfi*

Shakespeare: *Troilus and Cressida, The Winter's Tale*

Jonson: *The Alchemist; Volpone*

Marston: *The Malcontent*

COLLOQUIUM 3

Donne: *Songs and Sonnets*

Bacon: *Novum Organum*

Descartes: *Meditations*

Pascal: *Pensées*

Molière: *Tartuffe; The Misanthrope; The Physician in Spite of Himself; The Would-Be Gentleman*

Hume: *Dialogues Concerning Natural Religion; An Enquiry Concerning Human Understanding,* sections 1–7

Diderot: *Conversation between D'Alembert and Diderot; D'Alembert's Dream;* Supplement to Bougainville's *Voyage; Rameau's Nephew*

Rousseau: *Confessions,* books 1, 2, 5, 6, 8, 10

Sterne: *A Sentimental Journey through France and Italy*

Goethe: *The Sorrows of Young Werther; Faust*

Gibbon: *The Decline and Fall of the Roman Empire,* chapters 1, 2, 16, 17, 20, 23, 24, 31, 34, conclusion to chapter 38, 40, 50, 58, 68, 71

Hegel: *The Philosophy of History*

Kierkegaard: *Fear and Trembling; Sickness unto Death*

Stendhal: *The Charterhouse of Parma*

Wordsworth: *The Prelude*

COLLOQUIUM 4

Keats: "On First Looking into Chapman's Homer"; "The Eve of St. Agnes"; "Ode to a Nightingale"; "Ode to a Grecian Urn"; "Ode to Psyche"; "To Autumn"; "Ode to Melancholy"; "Hyperion"; "Bright Star . . ."

Flaubert: *Sentimental Education*

Arnold: "Dover Beach"; "Stanza from the Grande Chartreuse"; Preface to *Essays in Criticism; The Function of Criticism; The Study of Poetry; Wordsworth; Culture and Anarchy*

Twain: *Huckleberry Finn*

Tolstoi: *Anna Karenina*

Dostoevsky: *The Brothers Karamazov*

Nietzsche: *Birth of Tragedy; Beyond Good and Evil*

Shaw: *The Doctor's Dilemma; Caesar and Cleopatra; St. Joan*

Trotsky: *History of the Russian Revolution*

Freud: *Civilization and Its Discontents; Beyond the Pleasure Principle*

Mann: *Death in Venice;* "Mario and the Magician"; "Disorder and Early Sorrow"; *Confessions of Felix Krull; Tonio Kröger*

Kafka: *The Metamorphosis; The Trial*

Proust: *Swann's Way*

Yeats: *The Tower*

FINE ARTS AND MUSIC HUMANITIES

We have discussed the Fine Arts and Music humanities on page 56. Since the two courses rely heavily on visual and aural experiences, and try to cultivate the capacity to look at and listen to works of art, the reading lists are less important than the series of lectures and discussions conducted with slides and other visual and auditory materials. We include the basic outline for the structured discussions, but the various teachers allocate widely differing amounts of time to the different topics.

FINE ARTS

READING ASSIGNMENTS

Jerry J. Pollitt, *Art and Experience in Classical Greece,* chapter 3

Robert Branner, *Gothic Architecture,* pages 10–20

Emil Mâle, *The Gothic Image,* pages 1–22

Frederick Hartt, *History of Italian Renaissance Art,* for reference

Howard Hibbard, *Michelangelo,* for reference

H. Arthur Klein, *The Graphic Worlds of Pieter Bruegel,* for illustrations

Leo Bronstein, *El Greco,* for illustrations

Howard Hibbard, *Bernini,* chapter 1

Jakob Rosenberg, *Rembrandt,* sections on life and self-portraits (chapter 1 and beginning of chapter 2)

Phoebe Pool, *Impressionism,* for illustrations

John Golding, *Cubism,* illustrations and chapter 2 for reference

Vincent Scully, *Frank Lloyd Wright*

LECTURE AND DISCUSSION TOPICS

Some aesthetic concepts

1. Elements of visual form and therefore of analysis: line, mass, space, light and dark, color, texture.
2. Composition—the interrelation of these elements.
3. Relation of material to design.
4. Some factors affecting the style of works of art—place, time, personality.

The Parthenon, Athens (447–32 B.C.)

1. The building. The Parthenon on the Acropolis, dedicated to Athena Parthenos. Designed by Ictinus and Callicrates during the time of Pericles, of exceptional size (c. 225' x 100'). Subsequent history of the building. Its sculpture supervised by Phidias.

2. Purpose of the building.

3. Space problems of the Parthenon, internal and external—post and lintel (beam) construction.

4. Effect of light and shade.

5. Relation of material to design.

6. The Doric order: some of its parts—base, shaft, capital, echinus, abacus, entablature, architrave, frieze (triglyphs and metopes), cornice, pediments.

7. Refinements: taper and entasis of column shafts, inclination and displacement of columns, horizontal curvature.

8. Metopes: Centaurs and Lapiths (Greeks); light and shade; their design as related to the building and within the separate slabs.

9. Inner frieze—Panathenaic procession (all-Athenian): location, technique (low relief or bas relief), design.

10. Pediments: east pediment—*Birth of Athena* (Helios), Demeter, Persephone, Selene; identification problems with order of figures; west pediment—*Contest of Athena and Poseidon* (Cephissus, Ilissus); anthropomorphism; design of pediments.

11. Style of Parthenon sculpture, "canon of proportions."

12. Analogies of sculpture, architecture, and literature.

Amiens Cathedral

1. Amiens Cathedral, built chiefly between 1220–69, designed by Robert de Lusarches, Thomas de Cormont, and Renaud de Cormont. Built of limestone, 470' length, 213' total width, 137' to crown (apex) of vault.

2. Position in community.

3. Plan: cruciform; orientation; parts of plan—nave, aisles, transepts, crossing, choir, apse with principal altar, ambulatory, radiating chapels.

4. Arch and vault construction: four-part vault, ribs, piers with vaulting shafts, tower, and flying buttresses.

5. Internal and external design—nave arcade, triforium, clearstory, facade (west end).

6. Relations to space.

7. Location of sculptures.

8. Subject matter of sculpture in west portals: trumeau figures: Saint Firmin, Beau Dieu (Christ), and Virgin; *Last Judgement* in tympanum; quatrefoils with *Labors of the Months, Signs of the Zodiac,* and *Virtues and Vices.*

9. *Design and style of sculpture.*

Raphael (1483–1520)

1. Life: born Urbino, then a minor center of the Renaissance; trained by Giovanni Santi (his father), Timoteo Viti, influenced by Perugino and Leonardo da Vinci; worked in Florence 1504–8, in Rome 1508–20 for Popes Julius II and Leo X.

2. Tempera medium: wood panel, gesso (plaster), egg.

3. Linear and atmospheric perspective: foreshortening, chiaroscuro, contrapposto.

4. *Marriage of the Virgin* (5'6" x 3'9"); *Madonna del Cardellino* (3'5" x 2'5"); *Sistine Madonna* (8'8" x 6'5", Saint Sixtus and Saint Barbara).

5. *Baldassare Castiglione* (2'8" x 2'2"); *Leo X and Cardinals* (5' x 3'10").

6. Fresco (painting on wet plaster); cartoon; pouncing.

7. *Camera della Segnatura,* 1508–11, in the Vatican, Rome (palace of the Popes); *Disputa; School of Athens; Parnassus; Jurisprudence.*

8. *Camera d'Eliodoro; Miracle of Bolsena.*

Michelangelo Buonarroti (1475–1564)

1. Life: born Caprese, home of stone cutters; apprenticed to Ghirlandaio (1488), a Florentine painter known for his frescoes; studied collection of ancient sculpture in Medici gardens; religious spirit affected by Savonarola and by neoplatonism; worked chiefly in Florence and Rome.

2. Sculpture: *Pieta* (1498–1500, 5'9"); *David* (1501–3, 18'); tomb of Julius in San Pietro in Vincoli, Rome (1505–45) with *Bound Slaves* (7'6") and *Moses* (8'4"); Medici Tombs in New Sacristy of San Lorenzo, (1519–33) with *Giuliano di Medici, Night and Day, Lorenzo di Medici, Dusk and Dawn; Deposition* (c. 1550–56).

3. Frescoes in Sistine Chapel, Vatican, Rome: Ceiling (1508–12); *Creation of the World and of Man,* his fall and God's promise of redemption in stories of Noah and the Deluge; Libyan, Delphic, and other sibyls; Jeremiah, Ezekiel, Isaiah, Jonah, and other prophets; nude figures, (132' x 45'); *Last Judgement* on end wall (1535–41).

Peter Bruegel (c. 1525–69)

1. Life: born Brueghel, near Breda; to Italy, 1553; Antwerp, 1555–62; Brussels, 1563–69. Luther and the Protestant Reformation; Emperor

Charles V, Philip II of Spain, and Inquisition in the Netherlands.

2. Drawings for engravings: *Big Fish Eat Little Fish; Sloth; Justice; Temperance.*

3. Paintings: *Fall of Icarus* (29" x 44"); *Flemish Proverbs* (1599, 46" x 64"); *Carrying the Cross* (1564, 49" x 67").

4. Paintings: *The Seasons* (1565, each 46" x 63" or 64"); *Huntsmen in the Snow;* the *Dark Day;* the *Hay Harvest;* the *Harvesters; Return of the Herds.*

5. Paintings: *Flemish Kermess* (Peasant Dance 45" x 64"); *Peasant Wedding* (Harvest Festival, 45" x 64"); *The Land of Plenty* (1567, 20" x 31"); *Blind Leading the Blind* (1568, 34" x 61").

El Greco (Domenikos Theotokopoulos, 1541–1614)

1. The Catholic Counter-Reformation; Saint Ignatius Loyola, the Jesuit Order (1540).

2. Life: born Candia, Crete; in Venice studied with Titian and was also influenced by Tintoretto; in Rome, 1570; settled in Toledo, Spain, 1577.

3. Early paintings: *Purification of the Temple* (3'10" x 5'9"); *Assumption of the Virgin* (1577, 12'7" x 6'5").

4. Later religious paintings: *Martyrdom of Saint Maurice* (1581–84, 14'7" x 9'11"); *Burial of the Count of Orgaz* (1586, 15'9" x 11'9"); *Crucifixion; Ressurection* (9' x 4'2"); *Immaculate Conception* (1613, 10'7" x 5'6"); *Vision of Saint John.*

5. *Cardinal Nino de Guevara* (5'7" x 3'6").

6. *View of Toledo* (4' x 3'7").

Gian Lorenzo Bernini (1598–1680) and the Baroque

1. Life: born Naples, to Rome 1605; favorite artist of Pope Urban VIII (1623–44); lost and partially regained favor under Pope Innocent X (1644–55); favorite artist of Pope Alexander VII (1655–67), to Paris (1665) at invitation of Louis XIV.

2. Classical subject: *Apollo and Daphne* (1622–25).

3. Religious subjects: *David* (1623–24, 5'6"); *Saint Longinus* (1629–38, 16'4"); *Habakkuk and the Angel* (1655–61); *Ecstasy of Saint Theresa of Avila,* Cornaro Chapel, Sta. Maria della Vittoria (1645–52); *Death of the Blessed Ludovica Albertona* (1674).

4. Portraits: *Cardinal Scipone Borghese* (1632, 2'6"); *Constanza Buonarelli* (c. 1635); *Francesco d'Este* (1650–51); *Louis XIV* (1665).

5. Tombs: of Urban VIII (1628–47); of Alexander VII (1671–78).

6. Fountain: *Four Rivers fountain, Piazza Navona* (1648–51).

7. Architectural sculpture and architecture at St. Peter's: baldacchino (1624–33, 95'); Chair of St. Peter (1657–66); Piazza in front of St. Peter's (1656–67).

Rembrandt van Rijn (1606–69)

1. Dutch background and life: War of liberation from Catholic Spain (1568–1648); born Leyden, son of a prosperous miller; to Amsterdam, 1632; married Saskia van Uylenborch 1634, who died 1642; lived with Handrickje Stoffels 1649 to her death 1664?; bankrupt 1656; auctions 1657, 1658.

2. Religious paintings: *Presentation in the Temple* (1631, 24" x 19"); *Holy Family* (1646); *Supper at Emmaus.*

3. Portraits: Self portraits; *Saskia in a Red Hat* (38" x 30"); *Rembrandt and Saskia* (5'3" x 4'3"); *Rabbi* (29" x 25"); *Hendrickje at an Open Window* (34" x 25"); impasto; glazes.

4. Group Portraits: *Dr. Tulp's Anatomy Lesson* (1632, 5'5" x 7'2"); *Frans Banning Cocq's Company of the Civic Guard,* commonly called *The Night Watch* (1642, 11'9" x 14'3"); *Board of Governors of the Cloth Guild,* commonly called *The Syndics* (1661–62, 6'1" x 9').

5. Miscellaneous: *The Ruin; Stone Bridge; Carcass of Beef;* graphic arts: *The Crucifixion.*

Claude Monet (1840–1926); Auguste Renoir (1841–1919); and
Impressionism

1. *Terrace St. Adresse; Les Grands Boulevards; Dechargeurs de Charbon; Gare St. Lazare.*

2. *Haystacks; Bassin des Nympheas; Bridge at Argenteuil.*

3. *Artist's Garden; Seine at Giverny; Rouen Cathedral.*

4. Plein airisme: *Monet Painting* (Renoir); *Blanche Monet Painting.*

5. Broken color: *Portrait of a Girl* (Renoir); *Doge's Palace; Moulin de la Galette* (Renoir).

6. *Breakfast Table.*

Pablo Picasso (1881–1973)

1. *Absinthe Drinker; Old Guitarist* (1903); *Mother and Child; Les Demoiselles d'Avignon.*

2. Analytic Cubism: *Fernande* (1908); *Horta di Ebro* (1909); *Lady in a Mantilla* (1909); *Woman with a Mandolin* (1910); *The Poet* (1910); *Still Life* (1912).

3. Collage: *Still Life with Chair Caning* (1911); *The Student* (1914).

4. *Diaghilev and Selisburg* (1917); *Mme. Picasso* (1919); *Woman in White* (1923).

5. Synthetic Cubism: *Harlequin* (1918); *Dog and Cock* (1921); *Red Tablecloth* (1924); *Painter and Model* (1927); *Woman Before Mirror* (1932); *Guernica* (1937).

Frank Lloyd Wright (1867–1959)

1. Unity Temple (1905–06), Oak Park, Ill.
2. Larkin Building (1905), Buffalo, N.Y.
3. Coonley House (1908), Riverside, Ill.; Robie House (1909), Chicago.
4. Millard House (1921) (precast concrete blocks), Pasadena.
5. Kaufmann House (1936) (cantilever, reinforced concrete), Bear Run, Pa.
6. Johnson Wax Company Building (1939), Racine, Wis.

Music

READING ASSIGNMENTS

Libretto of Mozart's *Don Giovanni*

Libretto of Verdi's *Otello*

Gerald Abraham, *A Hundred Years of Music*

Willi Apel, *Harvard Dictionary of Music,* for reference

Baker's Biographical Dictionary of Musicians, for reference

David Boyden, *An Introduction to Music*

Beekman C. Cannon, Alvin H. Johnson, and William G. Waite, *The Art of Music*

Edward J. Dent, *Opera*

Donald J. Grout, *A History of Western Music*

Joseph Kerman, *Opera as Drama*

Paul H. Lang, *Music in Western Civilization*

Douglas Moore, *From Madrigal to Modern Music*

Carl Parrish and John F. Ohl, *Masterpieces of Music before 1750*

Oliver Strunk, *Source Readings in Music History*

LISTENING ASSIGNMENTS

Medieval and Renaissance

GREGORIAN CHANT

Hymn: *Exsultet orbis gaudiis,* and *Kyrie Altissime*

Gradual: *Protector noster,* and *Alleluia, Domine in virtute*

SECULAR MONOPHONIC MUSIC

Bernart de Ventadorn: *Can vei la lauzeta mover*

Guillaume de Machaut: *Douce dame jolie* (virelai)

ORGANUM

Rex caeli, Domine (parallel organum)

Benedicamus Domino (melismatic organum)

Perotinus: *Sederunt Principes*

SECULAR POLYPHONIC MUSIC

Thirteenth-century motet: *Ja n'amerai/ Sire Dieus*

Machaut: *Plus dure que un dyamant* (viralai)

RENAISSANCE MOTET

Jacob Obrecht: *Parce, Domine*

Cristobal de Morales: *Pastores dicite*

Tomás Luis de Victoria: *Pastores loquebantur*

RENAISSANCE MASS

Giovanni Pierluigi da Palestrina: *Gloria* from the Pope Marcellus Mass

Josquin Desprez: *Gloria* from the Pange Lingua Mass

FRENCH CHANSON

Clément Janequin: *La Guerre (La Bataille)*

ITALIAN MADRIGAL

Luca Marenzio: *Scaldava il sol*

Claudio Monteverdi: *Si ch'io vorrei morire*

ENGLISH MADRIGAL

John Wilbye: *Lady, When I Behold*

MUSIC FOR VOICE AND INSTRUMENT(S)

John Dowland: *My Ladye Hunsdon's Puffe;* song with lute, *In Darkness Let Me Dwell*

Heinrich Isaak: *La Mi La Sol*

Josquin Desprez: *La Bernadina*

Baroque and Classical

Claudio Monteverdi: *Orfeo* (1607), excerpt from Act II

G. F. Handel: *Acis and Galatea* (ca. 1720), Act II

J. S. Bach: *Wachet auf,* Cantata No. 140 (ca. 1731); *The Passion According to St. John* (1723), part 2 through the bass arioso "Betrachte, meine Seel"

G. F. Handel: Concerto Grosso, Opus 6, No. 9

J. S. Bach: Prelude and Fugue in D Minor, *Well-Tempered Clavier,* Book I, No. 6

Antonio Vivaldi: Violin Concerto, Opus 3, No. 12 (ca. 1712)

Selected Baroque suites and sonatas (to be performed)

Joseph Haydn: Symphony No. 102 (1794/95); String Quartet in C Major, Opus 76, No. 3 (1797/98)

Wolfgang Amadeus Mozart: Divertimento in B♭, K. 186 (1773); Piano Concerto in C Major, K. 503 (1786); Requiem Mass in D Minor (1791), *Dies irae* through *Recordare; Don Giovanni* (1787), Act I, through "Là ci darem"; Act I, "Or sai, chi l'onore" through finale; Act II, "Mi tradi" through finale

Ludwig van Beethoven: Symphony No. 7 (1812); String Quartet, Opus 95 (1810); Piano sonata (to be performed)

Romantic

Johannes Brahms: *Variations on a Theme by Haydn,* Opus 56a (1873)

Hector Berlioz: *Symphonie fantastique* (1830), last two movements

Richard Wagner: *Tristan und Isolde* (completed 1859), Act II, scene 2

Giuseppe Verdi: *Otello* (1887), Act I and beginning of Act II; conclusion of Act III and complete Act IV

Claude Debussy: "Minstrels," No. 12 in *Préludes,* Book I (1910); "Nuages," from *Nocturnes for Orchestra* (1893–99)

Richard Strauss: *Till Eulenspiegel* (1895)

Hugo Wolf: *Lebe wohl,* No. 36 in song collection *Gedichte von Mörike* (1888)

Gustav Mahler: "Ging heut' morgens," No. 2 in his *Lieder eines fahrenden Gesellen* (*Songs of a Wayfarer,* 1884)

Modern

Igor Stravinsky: *Le Sacre du Printemps* (1913), part 1; Octet (1923), second and third movements

Alban Berg: *Wozzeck* (1922), Act III

Béla Bartók: Music for Strings, Percussion, and Celesta (1937), first and second movements

Arnold Schoenberg; String Quartet No. 4, Opus 37 (1934), first movement

Anton Webern: Quartet, Opus 22 (1930), first movement

Elliott Carter: Sonata for Flute, Oboe, Cello, and Harpsichord (1952), first movement

Aaron Copland: *Rodeo* (1942), first movement

Charles Ives: *General Booth Enters Heaven* (1914)

Edgard Varèse: *Ionisation* (1931)

Paul Hindemith: *Mathis der Maler* (1934), first movement

ORIENTAL HUMANITIES

We have mentioned Oriental Humanities on page 59. As an elective sequel to the Western Humanities courses, Oriental Humanities introduces a body of material into the curriculum for nonspecialists which students and faculty members in many schools rarely encounter. We are therefore giving the reading list for this course in greater detail than those for our other humanities courses.

READINGS: NEAR EAST AND INDIA

For general reference: *A Guide to Oriental Classics.* New York: Columbia University Press, 1964.

TOPICS AND READING ASSIGNMENTS:

    I. A. *The Seven Odes.* Trans. by Arthur J. Arberry. New York: Macmillan, 1957. Poems, pp. 61–66, 83–89, 114–18, 142–47, 170–84, 204–9. For background, see pp. 13–22 and 249–54.

        B. *The Koran Interpreted.* Trans. by Arthur J. Arberry. New York: Macmillan, 1964. Suras 1, 2, 4, 9, 12, 16, 19, 23, 24, 33, 37, 49, 53, 56, 63, 68–114.

   II. A. Al-Hariri. *The Assemblies of Al-Hariri.* Trans. by T. Chenery and F. Steingass. London: Oriental Translation Fund, 1867–98. Preface and Assemblies 1, 2, 12, 23, 25, 31, 48–50.

        B. Avicenna. *Avicenna's Visionary Recital.* Trans. by Roger Trask from the French version of H. Corbin. New York: Pantheon Books, 1960.

(OR) Attar. *The Conference of the Birds.* Trans. C. S. Nott. London: Routledge and K. Paul, 1961.

III. A. Al-Ghazali. *Deliverance from Error, in the Faith and Practice of Al-Chazali.* Trans. by W. Montgomery Watts. London: Allen & Unwin, 1953.

   B. Averroes. *On the Harmony of Religion and Philosophy.* Trans. by George F. Hourani. London: Luzac & Co., 1961. Pp. 45–81.

IV. A. Ibn Khaldun. *The Muqaddimah: An Introduction to History.* Ed. and abridged by Dawood from the translation of Franz Rosenthal. Princeton: Princeton University Press, 1970.

   B. Rumi. *The Mystical Poems of Rumi.* Trans. by Arthur J. Arberry. Chicago: Chicago University Press, 1968. Poems 1, 7, 12, 16, 20, 28, 36, 46, 50, 59, 68, 80, 85, 86, 90, 101, 112, 119, 129, 144, 151, 170, 180, 191.

   ALTERNATIVE READING: Joseph Campbell, ed., *The Arabian Nights.* Viking Press.

V. A. *Selections from the Vedic Hymns.* Trans. by E. Daniel Smith. Berkeley: McCutchan, 1968.

   B. Chandogya, Brihadaranyaka, and Katha Upanishads. In Robert E. Hume, trans. *The Thirteen Principal Upanishads.* Oxford, Galaxy Paperback, 1971.

VI. A. *Buddhism in Translation.* Ed. by Henry C. Warren. New York: Atheneum, 1963. Pp. 1–95.

   B. *Buddhist Suttas.* Trans. by T. W. Rhys Davids. New York: Dover, 1963. Pp. 1–155.

   SUGGESTED READING: *The Buddhist Tradition.* Ed. by Wm. Theodore deBary et al. New York: Modern Library, 1969. Pp. 3–72.

VII. A. *Entering the Path of Enlightenment: The Bodhicaryavatara of the Buddhist Poet Santideva.* Trans. by Marion L. Matics. New York: Macmillan, 1970. Pp. 143–232.

   B. *The Diamond Sutra.* In *Buddhist Wisdom Books.* Trans. by Edward Conze. London: Allen & Unwin, 1958. Pp. 21–74.

   SUGGESTED READING: *The Buddhist Tradition.* Pp. 72–122.

VIII. A. *Mahabharata.* Trans. by Chakravarti V. Marasimhan. New York: Columbia University Press, 1965.

   (AND/OR) *The Mahabharata.* J.A.B. van Buitenen, trans. Vols. I and II. Chicago, 1973.

   B. *The Ramayana.* In *Ramayana and Mahabharata.* Trans. by C.

Dutt. New York: Dutton Everyman, 1955. Pp. 1–37, 54–65, 76–107, 117–52.

(OR) *Myths of the Hindus and Buddhists.* Ed. by Amanda Coomaraswamy Sr. Nivedita. Dover Paperback, n.d.

SUGGESTED READING: R. K. Narayan. *Gods, Demons, and Others.* New York: Viking, 1967.

IX. *The Bhagavad Gita.* Trans. by Franklin Edgerton. Torchbook, 1944.

X. A. Kalidasa. *Shakuntala.* In *Shakuntala and Other Writings.* Trans. by Arthur W. Ryder. New York: Dutton Everyman, 1959. Pp. 3–94.

B. Shudraka. *The Little Clay Cart.* In *Two Plays of Ancient India.* Trans. by J.A.B. van Buitenen. New York: Columbia University Press, 1968. Pp. 47–180.

XI. A. *A Sourcebook in Indian Philosophy.* Ed. by Saruepelli Radhakrishnan and Charles Moore. Princeton: Princeton University Press, 1968. Read chapter 15 on Vedanta.

B. "*The Yoga Sutra.*" Trans. by Royal Weiler. Library Mimeograph.

XII. A. Bhartrihari. *Bhartrihari: Poems.* Trans. by Barbara Stoler Miller. New York: Columbia University Press, 1967.

B. Kalidasa. *The Cloud Messenger.* Trans. by F. and E. Edgerton. Ann Arbor: University of Michigan Press, 1964.

C. In *Praise of Krishna.* Trans. by Edward C. Dimock and Denise Levertov. New York: Doubleday Anchor, 1967.

(OR) *Love Song of the Dark Lord: Jayadeva's Gitagovinda.* Trans. by Barbara Stoler Miller. New York: Columbia University Press, 1977

XIII. A. Tagor. *A Tagore Reader.* Ed. by A. Chakravarty. New York: Macmillan, 1961. Pp. 45–97, 115–223, 291–375.

B. Mohandas Gandhi. *An Autobiography: The Story of My Experiments with Truth.* Boston: Beacon, 1968, part 1; part 2: chaps. 5, 11, 22; part 3: chaps. 5–8; part 4: chaps. 6–7, 19–20, 26–31; part 5: chaps. 12–14, 23–25; "Farewell."

READINGS: CHINA AND JAPAN

For general reference:

A Guide to Oriental Classics, New York: Columbia University Press, 1964 (for additional translations, secondary readings, and suggested discussion topics).

The Classic Chinese Novel, by C. T. Hsia. New York: Columbia University Press, 1968.

TOPICS AND READING ASSIGNMENTS

   I. *The Analects of Confucius* Arthur Waley (trans.). New York: Modern Library. Pb.

  II. *Mencius,* W. A. C. Dobson (trans.). Toronto: University of Toronto Press, 1963. Pb.

   (OR) *Mencius,* D. C. Lau (trans.). Baltimore: Penguin Classics, 1970.

   Mo Tzu: Basic Writings, Burton Watson (trans.). New York: Columbia University Press, 1963. Pb. Pp. 18–22, 34–83, 94–116.

 III. *The Way and Its Power,* Arthur Waley (trans.). New York: Macmillan, 1957. Pp. 141–242.

   (AND/OR) *Lao Tzu: Tao Te Ching,* D. C. Lau (trans.). Baltimore: Penguin Classics, 1963.

   Chuang Tzu: Basic Writings, Burton Watson (trans.). New York: Columbia University Press, 1964. Pb.

  IV. *Hsun Tzu: Basic Writings,* Burton Watson (trans.). New York: Columbia University Press, 1963. Pb.

   Han Fei Tzu: Basic Writings, Burton Watson (trans.). New York: Columbia University Press, 1964. Pb. Pp. 16–48, 73–79, 96–129.

   V. *The Lotus Sutra* (abridged), W. E. Soothill (trans.), in *The Lotus of the Wonderful Law.* Oxford: Clarendon Press, 1929. Chs. 1–4, 10–12, 16.

   The Awakening of Faith, Yoshito Hakeda. New York: Columbia University Press, 1967.

   The Platform Sutra of the Sixth Patriarch, Philip Yampolsky (trans.). New York: Columbia University Press, 1967. Pp. 125–183.

  VI. *Monkey,* Arthur Waley (trans.). London: Allen & Unwin; New York: Grove Press, 1958.

   Chinese Poems, Arthur Waley (trans.). London: Allen & Unwin, 1964. Pb.

   (OR) *Poems of the Late T'ang,* A. G. Graham (trans.). Baltimore: Penguin Classics, 1965.

   (OR) *Su Tung-p'o,* Burton Watson (trans.). New York: Columbia University Press, 1965.

(OR) "Chinese Poems." Library Mimeograph.

VII. *A Source Book in Chinese Philosophy,* Wing-tsit Chan (ed.). Princeton: Princeton University Press, 1967. Pp. 388–691.

Reflections on Things at Hand, Wing-tsit Chan. New York: Columbia University Press, 1967. Pp. 123–53, 289–308.

Instructions for Practical Learning, Wing-tsit Chan. New York: Columbia University Press, 1963. Pp. 117–24, 271–80, 298–306.

SUBSTITUTE: *Records of the Historian,* San-ma Ch'ien (trans. by Burton Watson). New York: Columbia University Press, 1969. Pb.

VIII. *The Dream of the Red Chamber,* C. C. Wang (trans.). New York: Doubleday Anchor, 1958. Pb.

(OR) *The Dream of the Red Chamber,* F. I. McHugh (trans.). New York: Pantheon Books, 1958.

Romance of the Western Chamber, H. I. Hsiung (trans.). New York: Columbia University Press, 1968.

IX. *The Travels of Lao Ts'an,* Harold Shadick (trans.). Ithaca: Cornell University Press, 1952. Pb.

SUBSTITUTE: "Buddhism in Japan" Wm. Theodore de Bary (ed.), in *The Buddhist Tradition.* New York: Modern Library, 1968. Pp. 255-398.

X. *The Tale of Genji,* Murasaki Shikibu (trans. by Arthur Waley). New York: Modern Library Giant, n.d. Pp. 3–357 (and pp. 747–1135).

XI. *The Pillow Book of Sei Shonagon,* Ivan Morris (trans.). New York: Columbia University Press, 1967.

"An Account of my Hut," Kamo no Chomei (Donald Keene, trans.) in *Anthology of Japenese Literature,* Donald Keene (ed.). New York: Grove Press, 1955. Pb.

Essays in Idleness: The Tsurszuregusa of Kenko, Donald Keene (trans.). New York: Columbia University Press, 1967.

Japanese poetry in Keene *Anthology.*

XII. *20 Plays of the No Theater,* Donald Keene (ed.). New York: Columbia University Press 1970. Pb.

An Introduction to Haiku, H. Henderson. New York: Doubleday Anchor, 1958. Pp. 15–51.

"The Narrow Road to Oku," Matsuo Basho (Donald Keene, trans.) in *Anthology.* Pp. 363–85.

XIII. *Four Major Plays of Chikamatsu,* Donald Keene (trans.). New York: Columbia University Press, 1963. Pb.

Five Women Who Loved Love, Iharu Saikaku (Wm. Theodore de Bary, trans.). Rutland, Vt.: Charles E. Tuttle, 1965. Pb.

(OR) *Life of an Amorous Woman,* Ivan Morris (trans.). New York: New Directions, 1967.

⟫ Contemporary Civilization ⟪

CONTEMPORARY CIVILIZATION IN THE WEST

As we mentioned on page 62, the readings for the Contemporary Civilization courses have changed more, over a longer time, than those for Humanities. In the 1950s, the readings for the courses were gathered into two large volumes which are listed below. These volumes consist largely of passages from original sources, sometimes only a page or two, sometimes more than twenty pages. In addition, they contain essays, introductions, and connecting material by members of the Columbia staff or other experts. The chapter on the medieval heritage, for example, contains documents relating to several institutions and ideological stands of the Middle Ages:

The Medieval Heritage: Economy, Society, Polity; The Manor; The Town; The Ordinance of Laborers; Grant of Two Fairs at Aix-La-Chapelle; The Kings Mirror; Robert of Clari; Innocent III; Genoese Shipping; Saint Thomas Aquinas; Las Siete Partidas; The Goliard Poets; Magna Carta.

A companion volume, *Chapters in Western Civilization*, contains essays written by scholars in the field to accompany the documents. Below we give a sample on the Middle Ages.

I. THE HERITAGE OF THE ANCIENT WORLD
   Henri Marrou, *Sorbonne*

II. MEDIEVAL THOUGHT: CHRISTIAN CONCEPTIONS OF LIFE.
   Kenneth Scott Latourette, *Yale University*

III. THE GROWTH OF LEARNING IN THE WEST.
   Marshall Clagett, *University of Wisconsin*

IV. EUROPEAN SOCIETY IN THE MIDDLE AGES.
   John Hine Mundy, *Columbia University*

V. THE MEDIEVAL ECONOMY.
   Marshall Clagett, *University of Wisconsin*

VI. MEDIEVAL POLITICAL INSTITUTIONS.
Joseph R. Strayer, *Princeton University*

Introduction to Contemporary Civilization in the West. 2d ed. Vols. 1 and 2. New York: Columbia University Press, 1954.
Chapters in Western Civilization. 3d ed. New York: Columbia University Press, 1961.

CONTEMPORARY CIVILIZATION IN THE WEST AFTER 1960

In the late 1960s the availability of paperbacks and the increased specialization among social science teachers led the Contemporary Civilization staff to return to a list of separate books for its reading. At present each teacher selects a set of books from a larger list. In recent years the overlap between the different sections of the course taught by representatives of different disciplines has been increasing.

READINGS FOR ORIENTAL CIVILIZATION

As an elective course designed to give general education to students who may never specialize in the oriental field, the Oriental Civilization courses must deal with an enormous diversity of texts and traditions. For the Islamic tradition no anthology has yet been published, although one is in preparation. For the Oriental Civilization courses we list the anthologies which constitute the syllabus for the course.

Sources of Indian Tradition. Compiled by Wm. Theodore de Bary, Stephen Hay, Royal Weiler, and Andrew Yarrow. New York: Columbia University Press, 1958.
Sources of Chinese Tradition. Compiled by Wm. Theodore de Bary, Wing-tsit Chan, and Burton Watson. New York and London: Columbia University Press, 1960.
Sources of Japanese Tradition. Compiled by Ryusaku Tsunoda, Wm.

Theodore de Bary, and Donald Keene. New York: Columbia University Press, 1958.

Sources of the Islamic Tradition, to be published by Columbia University Press (in preparation).

⇶ Seminar Reports ⇶

We list below the topics and speakers which have made up our Thursday noon meetings for the past three and one-half years. Copies of the talks are available from the Office of the Program in General Education, 1513 School of International Affairs, Columbia University, New York 10027.

Volume I (1973–74)

No. 1: "General Education and the Humanities," by Wm. Theodore de Bary, *Executive Vice-President for Academic Affairs, and Provost, Columbia.*

No. 2: "Humanities, Pieties, Practicalities, Universities," by Jacques Barzun, *University Professor Emeritus, Columbia;* "The Mind Without Walls—or Roof," by Robert Gorham Davis, *Professor of English, Columbia.*

No. 3: "A Second Look at General Education," by Daniel Bell, *Professor of Sociology, Harvard, University;* "General Education and the American Preparatory System" by Lionel Trilling, *University Professor, Columbia.*

No. 4: "Thoughts on Teaching Science to Non-Specialists," by Gerald Feinberg, *Professor of Physics, Columbia;* "The Chemistry Program at Columbia," by Ronald C. Breslow, *Samuel Latham Mitchill Professor of Chemistry, Columbia.*

No. 5: "General Education, Innovation, and an Undergraduate Curriculum," by Peter R. Pouncey, *Dean of Columbia College;* "Values, Techniques, and Secondary Consequences," by Ivar Berg, *George E. Warren Professor of Business, Columbia;* "History as an Interdisciplinary Discipline," by Peter Gay, *Durfee Professor of History, Yale University;* "A Business School View of General Education and the Humanities," by James W. Kuhn, *Professor of Industrial Relations, Columbia.*

No. 6: "Religious Studies and General Education at Columbia," by Paul R. Valliere, *Assistant Professor of Religion, Columbia;* "General Education in an Industrial Economy," by Mortimer J. Adler, *Director, Encyclopedia Britannica;* "The Relationship between Legal Education and the Arts and Sciences," by R. Kent Greenawalt,

Telford Taylor, and Charles Frankel, *Professors, Columbia University Law School.*

No. 7: "General Education in a Technological Society," by Ralph J. Schwarz and Mario G. Salvadori, *Professors, Columbia University School of Engineering;* "The Architecture of Humanism," by James S. Polshek and Kenneth Frampton, *Professors, Columbia University School of Architecture.*

No. 8: "Arts Education for Undergraduates," by Bernard Beckerman, *Professor of Dramatic Arts, Columbia;* "Interdisciplinary and Transdisciplinary Studies in the Humanities," by Henry D. Aiken, *Professor of Philosophy, Brandeis University;* "Health and Human Values: A Case Presentation," by Bernard Schoenberg and Allen I. Hyman, *Columbia University College of Physicians and Surgeons;* "General Education at the University of Chicago," by Leonard B. Meyer, *Professor of Music, University of Chicago.*

Volume 2 (1974–75)

No. 1: "Renaissance Studies," by Robert Hanning and David Rosand, *Professors of English and Art History, Columbia.*

No. 2: "Education for Diplomacy," by Abba Eban, *Visiting Professor, School of International Affairs, Columbia;* "Social Work and Social Policy," by Vera Shlakman and Mitchell I. Ginsberg, *School of Social Work, Columbia.*

No. 3: "An Interdisciplinary Approach to Problems of Human Behavior: B. F. Skinner and Noam Chomsky on Language," by Herbert S. Terrace and Arthur C. Danto, *Professors of Psychology and Philosophy, Columbia.*

No. 4: "J. Robert Oppenheimer: The Man and His Case," by Fred W. Friendly and Michael G. Wood, *Professors of Journalism and English, Columbia.*

No. 5: "Interdisciplinary Education: Role Strains and Adaptations," by Bernard Schoenberg et al.

No. 6: "Science and the Literary Imagination," by M. E. Bowen, J. A. Mazzeo et al., *Department of English, Columbia.*

No. 7: "The Impact of Economics on Industrial Technology," by Seymour Melman, *Professor of Industrial Engineering, Columbia;* "Metals: An Endangered Species?" by John K. Tien, *Professor of Metallurgy, Columbia.*

No. 8: "Learning as an Acquired Skill," by Marvin Minsky, *Donner Professor of Science, M.I.T.;* "The Impact of Computers on Society," by Cyrus Levinthal and Bruce Gilchrist, *Professors of Biology and Electrical Engineering, Columbia;* "The Sociology of Golden Ages," by Robert A. Nisbet, *Albert Schweitzer Professor of the Humanities, Columbia.*

Volume 3 (1975–76)

No. 1: "What Is a Profession?" by Walter P. Metzger, *Professor of History, Columbia.*

No. 2: "The Legal Profession's Need for a Human Commitment," by Curtis J. Berger, *Lawrence A. Wien Professor of Real Estate Law, Columbia;* "Professional Standards and Humane Values in the Practice of Law," by Saul Touster, *Professor of Law and Social Sciences, City University of New York,* and Richard G. Moser, *Chairman, Special Committee on Judicial Ethics, New York State Bar Association.*

No. 3: "The Professional School View of Liberal Education," by James A. Thomas, *Dean of Admissions, Yale Law School,* and Frederick G. Hofmann, *Associate Dean of Admissions, Columbia College of Physicians and Surgeons.*

No. 4: "Manpower Needs: Are Universities Training the Right People for the Right Jobs?" by Eli Ginzberg, *Hepburn Professor of Economics, Columbia;* "Professional Education and the Public Interest," by Jonathan Messerli, *Dean of The School of Education, Fordham University,* and Jonas F. Soltis, *Professor of Philosophy and Education, Teachers College;* "Training Graduate Students for Their Professional Careers," by Alfred Frazer et al., *Professors of Art History, Columbia.*

No. 5: "Role of the School of Architecture and Planning," by James Polshek, *Dean of Architecture, Columbia;* "Philosophy of the Urban Planning Division," by Peter Marcuse, *Professor of Urban Planning, Columbia;* "Values and the University: A Discussion," by David Sidorsky, *Professor of Philosophy, Columbia.*

No. 6: "Professionalization," by William J. Goode and Robert K. Merton, *Professors of Sociology, Columbia.*

No. 7: "Social Control & Medical Professionals," by Eliot Freidson, Bernard Barber, *Professors of Sociology, Columbia,* Lowell E. Bellin, *New York Commissioner of Health,* and John Colombotos, *Professor of Public Health, Columbia.*

No. 8: "Death and Professional Responsibility," by Paul Ramsey, *Paine Professor of Religion, Princeton University,* Frank P. Grad, *Pro-*

fessor of Law, Columbia, Samuel Klagsbrun, *Assistant Clinical Professor in Psychiatry, Columbia,* and Donald Shriver, *President, Union Theological Seminary.*

Thursday Seminars, Spring 1976

1. "Is Science For Poets?" Samuel Devons, *Professor of Physics, Columbia.*

2. History of Science in the University Curriculum" Loren Graham, *Professor of History, Columbia.*

3. "Educating Scientists and the Public for New Developments in Medical Science" James Darnell, *Astor Professor of Molecular Cell Biology, Rockefeller University.*

4. "Engineering and Humane Values" Mario Salvadori, *Renwick Professor Emeritus of Civil Engineering, Columbia.*

Thursday Seminars, Fall 1976

1. "Intellectual Foundations of Liberalism" Charles Frankel, *Old Dominion Professor of Philosophy and Public Affairs, Columbia.*

2. "Liberalism and Liberal Education: The Good Life and the Making of the Good Man" Thomas F. Green, *Professor of Education, Syracuse University.*

3. "Liberal Education and Western Humanism" Paul O. Kristeller, *Frederick J. E. Woodbridge Professor Emeritus of Philosophy, Columbia.*

4. "Religion and Humanism: The Decline of the Confrontation between Religion and Humanism in Higher Jewish Education" Gerson Cohen, *Chancellor, Jewish Theological Seminary;* "How Shall We Believe in Ourselves?" Donald Shriver, *President, Union Theological Seminary.*

5. "Aspects of American Character and Liberalism" Nathan I. Huggins, *Professor of History, Columbia.*

6. "Liberalism and Liberal Education in India" Rajni Kothari, *Wallach Professor of Political Science, Columbia,* Ainslie Embree, *Associate Dean, School of International Affairs, Columbia.*

7. "Chinese Humanism and Liberal Education: Mao and Confucius as the 'Great Teachers' of China" Wm. Theodore de Bary, *Horace Walpole Carpentier Professor of Oriental Studies, Columbia;* C. T. Hu, *Professor of Comparative Education, Teachers College.*

8. "Japan and Liberal Education" Wm. Theodore de Bary, Carol N. Gluck, *Lecturer, East Asian Languages and Cultures, Columbia,* Yoshito S. Hakeda, *Professor of Japanese, Columbia.*

9. "Liberalism in Russia" Leopold Haimson, *Professor of History; Col-*

umbia, Robert L. Belknap, *Professor of Russian Language and Literature, Columbia,* Paul R. Valliere, *Assistant Professor of Religion, Columbia.*

⇉ Professional School Seminars ⇇

We have described the Professional School Seminars on pages 68ff. The different arts-science and professional school leaders of these seminars organized them in various ways, but the seminar on Housing in the School of Architecture exhibits most of the elements of this group of courses. The seminars used staff from various parts of the university and experts from outside to cover a variety of topics with real expertise, sometimes addressed to students in the seminars, and sometimes, as shown below, for a wider audience. Students gathered in separate groups to bring their educational backgrounds to bear on the problems that were discussed in the lectures listed below.

GRADUATE SCHOOL OF ARCHITECTURE AND PLANNING

AMERICAN PUBLIC HOUSING SINCE THE NEW DEAL
(Architecture A4418y)

SPEAKERS HEARD AT PUBLIC SESSIONS

"Beyond the Rent Strike: The Aftermath of Pruitt-Igoe" Thomas Costello, *Executive Director, St. Louis Housing Authority,* Anita Miller, *Urban Program Officer, Ford Foundation.*

"The Future for New Housing: a New York Perspective" Edward Logue, *Former Executive Director, N.Y.S. Urban Development Corporation.*

"Subsidized Housing Since 1934: Its Impact on the People It Housed" Elizabeth Wood, *Former Executive Director, Chicago Housing Authority.*

"New Directions in Housing: The Work of SAR in Holland" John Habraken, *Professor of Architecture, Massachusetts Institute of Technology.*

"Housing and Social Policy: Realities of the Housing Allowance" Chester Hartman, *Urban Planning Consultant.*

CORE SESSIONS

Columbia faculty participants: J. Leavitt (*Urban Planning*); S. Lefkowitz (*Law*); P. Marcuse (*Urban Planning*); A. Medioli (*Urban Planning*); L. Mullings (*Anthropology*); R. Plunz (*Architecture*); W. Rich (*Political Science*); and B. Stevens (*Business*).

Weekly "core" sessions provided basic course material.

A Historical Perspective on Low Rental Apartment Building in Manhattan

A historical evaluation contrasting public and private panaceas for housing low-income families in Manhattan in the last century, with an emphasis placed on the mechanisms used for regulation of housing production.

Anthony Jackson, *Professor of Architecture, Nova Scotia Technical College.*

The Evolution of Housing Form as Institution

The evolution of U.S. urban housing form in relation to government regulation and architectural innovation; cost, ideological, and spatial factors which influence the forms of physical containment in housing.

Richard Plunz, *Associate Professor of Architecture, Columbia.*

Current Patterns of Housing Subsidy Allocation

Description and comparison of existing housing subsidy programs with an evaluation of their effectiveness in meeting housing need; the relative impact of each on the construction industry, the owner, and the tenant; the long-term impact of each on financial markets.

Barbara Stevens, *Assistant Professor of Business, Columbia.*

The Ideologies of Ownership and Property Rights

Analysis of tenure in housing; the legal, social, and economic relationships pursuant to which individual occupancy takes place; conceptual components of these relationships, with their ideological and direct implications; evaluation of public policy toward tenure.

Peter Marcuse, *Professor of Urban Planning, Columbia.*

The Cultural Environment of Public Housing

A historical and cross-cultural approach to the interrelationships of spatial environment and social structure; an examination of the way in which the environment of public housing influences social relations.

Leith Mullings, *Assistant Professor of Anthropology, Columbia.*

Benevolence and Self-Interest in the Formation of Housing Policy.

Examination of the history of public programs in housing, with an emphasis on the interests served, and an analysis of the immediate and long-range forces leading to their adoption.

Peter Marcuse, *Professor of Urban Planning, Columbia.*

Public Housing as a Vehicle for Political Manipulation

Analysis of the use of housing projects to mobilize political support; the role of the political party in the resocialization of new urban immigrants; the political efficiencies inherent to the housing project.

Wilbur Rich, *Assistant Professor of Political Science, Columbia.*

Suburban Reinforcement of Urban Housing Patterns

Examination of current legal forces used to reinforce existing suburban residency patterns; the effects of suburban no-growth policies on inner city populations; examination of recent court cases.

Stephen Lefkowitz, *Assistant Professor of Law, Columbia.*

Tenant Accountability and Patterns of Socialization

Description of patterns of learned behavior among tenants of housing projects; modes of tenant organization and expression; the role of the peer group in tenant resocialization.

Wilbur Rich, *Assistant Professor of Political Science, Columbia.*

Individual Tenant Preferences and Market Availability

Analysis of relative costs of various housing amenities compared with their value as measured by existing demand studies; programmatic constraints on meeting tenant demands; vicious circles in filling needs and filling demands.

Barbara Stevens, *Assistant Professor of Business, Columbia.*

Alternatives for Development Packaging

Examination of the principles of structuring development financing; interrelationships between the requirements for land occupancy, financing, and architect.

Stephen Lefkowitz, *Assistant Professor of Law, Columbia.*

Tenant Alternatives to Traditional Public Housing

Evaluation of rehabilitation profiles for selected housing settings in the private sector; analysis of issues concerning tenant management and tenant organization for low-income tenants who seek shelter outside of the public housing supply.

Jacqueline Leavitt, *Lecturer in Urban Planning, Columbia;* Alfred Medioli, *Graduate Assistant in Urban Planning, Columbia University.*

Issues of Equity in Public Housing Supports

The "culture of poverty" perspective and public housing; issues of ethnicity and economic stratification; who benefits from and who pays for housing programs; the impact of nonhousing programs on housing.

    Peter Marcuse, *Professor of Urban Planning, Columbia;* Leith Mullings, *Assistant Professor of Anthropology, Columbia.*

Public Housing Programs in Europe

Description of subsidy approaches in Europe in comparison to the U.S. with an emphasis on relative sizes and impact on owner, builder, and tenant; analysis of the flexibility of programs in Europe and U.S.

    Barbara Stevens, *Assistant Professor of Business, Columbia.*

The Proceedings are in preparation and will be published in Spring 1977 under the title *A Reader on American Public Housing: Working Paper 2.* Graduate School of Architecture and Planning.

In addition several studio and "working" sessions were scheduled to permit less formal exposure to housing issues.

SPECIAL STUDIO OPTION:

Low-Rise Infill Housing on Public Housing Tower Sites in Manhattan

The design studio option is open to all architecture students who are simultaneously enrolled in Architecture A4418y. Both courses focus on the physical and social issues which have been generated by American Public Housing programs. Participants study several existing Public Housing projects in Manhattan. Each project is analyzed in relation to a variety of physical and social criteria, in an attempt to determine the strengths and weakness of the planning and design. In addition, proposals will be formulated for the redesign of each project.

The sites are Taft Houses, Franklin Houses, Carver Houses, Baruch Houses, and Mitchel Houses. Each contains large open spaces, to be redeveloped through introduction of new low-rise, infill housing. This new housing can reincorporate the existing towers into the surrounding neighborhoods. A fine-grain neighborhood structure will be reestablished, with an emphasis on maximizing the benefits of ground-related organization. The New York City Housing Authority provides site data and other assistance.

Seminar sessions are coordinated with studio discussions, and seminar lecturers serve as studio consultants whenever possible. Scheduled presentations of studio work are open to all seminar students and faculty.

WORKING SESSION

New York City Housing Authority. John Simon, General Manager, met with seminar participants at the Fulton Senior Center, 119 Ninth Avenue.

Jersey City Housing Authority. Seminar participants met with Robert Rigby, Executive Director, in his office at the Hudson Gardens housing project.

Beekman Rehabs. Fieldtrip to Jose de Diego/Beekman Rehabs, South Bronx.

Brownsville. Fieldtrip to Brownsville and Van Dyck Houses (NYCHA) and Riverbend (HDA).

⇾⇾ The University Seminars ⇽⇽

We have described the University Seminars on page 58. As our most active institution for postdoctoral education, the University Seminars have a special structure and a special constitution. We append the constitution, written by Frank Tannenbaum in 1945, and follow it with a list of the University Seminars operating today.

CONSTITUTION, UNIVERSITY SEMINARS

1. The University Seminars are voluntary groups of Columbia faculty and off-campus specialists from academic and non-academic institutions gathered together in joint pursuit of knowledge in some specially designated area—such as The Renaissance, Peace, Ecological Systems and Cultural Evolution, Hermeneutics, etc., etc.
2. The University accepts the off-campus members of the University Seminars on the nomination of the seminar and appoints them University Seminar Associates without pay.
3. Each seminar selects its members as it needs them from wherever they may be available.
4. Each separate seminar is conceived of as a continuing association with lifelong fellows.
5. Each seminar picks its officers, formulates its program, and decides for itself the number of times it will meet during the month.
6. Neither members nor officers receive any emolument for their services to the seminars, nor pay any dues for membership.
7. Only rapporteurs and/or secretaries are paid regularly.
8. Associates who come from beyond Greater New York may be reimbursed for their travel expenses—usually limited to no more than $50 per associate for each separate meeting.
9. Associates and members pay for own food and hotel if they have to stay over night.
10. Only the speaker may receive both travel, food, and hotel expenses; the secretaries at the meetings have their dinners paid for them.

11. No rule of retirement applies to either members, associates, or officers of the seminars. An increasing number of retired members of the faculty are active participants in the Seminars.

12. Each of these separate seminars is accepted as "an independent universe" inside of the University, without interference as long as it abides within the broad limits of the academic tradition, free to pursue its intellectual involvement.

13. In the pursuit of their intellectual involvement, seminars have published books, circulated their proceedings, held joint meetings with each other, or with off-campus scientific institutions like the Rockefeller Institute; have established formal relations with another university, in this case the Aristotelian Center of Padua all of whose members are University Seminar Associates and members of the Renaissance Seminar are honorary members of the Aristotelian Center of Padua. The Seminar on The Renaissance and the Aristotelian Center at Padua have a joint publication program, at least three volumes have been published to date. Seminars have had and have in attendance students working for their doctorate, have organized research, accepted grants from foundations—The National Science Foundation, Naval Research, UNESCO—and have other diverse activities congenial to their needs—a bibliographical project by the Seminar on The Renaissance and public meetings at Arden House by the Seminar on The Economics of Distribution.

14. The University has followed the rule accepted at the beginning of this enterprise: of no interference in the life of the Seminars, leaving them in complete freedom to pursue their course as their needs dictated. Officers of the University elected to membership in a seminar are there as academic colleagues.

15. The University has reserved the right to excommunication, expulsion and denial of its name whenever it felt that any or all of the seminars were overstepping the bounds of the academic tradition, bringing discredit upon it, and misusing its good name.

16. The present Director received his charge from the Joint Committee on Graduate Instruction when he was elected chairman of the University Seminars soon after they were established. It was 17 years later, after retiring from the Department of History, that he asked for an appointment from the President because that was the only way he could have an office within the University from which to administer the seminars.

17. The Director has maintained continued contact with the members and officers of the various seminars and minor problems that have arisen

have always been settled so as to favor the work of, and maintain the interest and good will of, these developing institutions.

18. The University administration has always responded favorably to the demands made upon it by the University Seminars; these demands have not been numerous or burdensome.

19. The University has, from the beginning, given limited financial support to the seminars. They are now receiving $10,000. They will spend between $40,000 and $50,000 this year. The Director has always raised the difference somehow, usually in small amounts.

20. The University has not attempted to make rules for the way this money was spent—and we were free to use it for whatever the seminars required in the pursuit of their work—even for the dinner of the Ambassador and his lady when they were invited to the final meeting of one of the area Seminars.

21. These and many other rules have grown up in response to the request of the seminars and the aim has always been to relieve the officers of the seminars from undue administrative work and to provide what seemed useful to them within the limits of our income. On the average a University Seminar costs about $1,200 a year.

22. One illustration of how completely flexible the administration of the seminars is and has to be is illustrated by the following incident. The African Seminar, in arranging its final three meetings of the year 1965, was invited by one of its members to hold one meeting in his house where he has a widely-known collection of African art. He also agreed to talk that evening about African art and illustrate his talk with objects from his own collection. But he lives in Hartsdale. How was the seminar going to get there and who would pay for the transportation? The director was appealed to and he agreed to pay for automobile transportation for the members from the Faculty Club after dinner. The invitation had not included dinner. The members of the Seminar were delighted and enthusiastic. A refusal would have cast a damper upon this perfectly remarkable seminar which has done so much to increase interest in African studies at Columbia.

23. Each seminar at one time or another has its special needs and problems and the policy of the Seminar administration is, as far as possible within the limits imposed by income, to provide for each seminar a congenial and friendly environment within which to work.

24. The Annual Dinner to which all participants are invited has added an important element of companionship and common identity amongst the members and associates of the various seminars and helped to

maintain the feeling of friendship and good will so important to a voluntary association.

These are some of the elements of the unwritten consensus within which the Seminars have grown and expanded. They cannot all be put down on paper because they involve an attitude, a psychological relationship within the Seminar movement itself, between them and the Director, and between the seminars and the University. Our problem is how to preserve this into the future.

Respectfully submitted.

PROFESSOR FRANK TANNENBAUM
Director of University Seminars

UNIVERSITY SEMINARS, 1975–1976, COLUMBIA UNIVERSITY

(These are ongoing Seminars—the date following the name of each Seminar indicates the year it was founded.)

THE STATE (1945)

THE PROBLEM OF PEACE (1945)

STUDIES IN RELIGION (1945)

THE RENAISSANCE (1945)

CONTENT AND METHODS OF THE SOCIAL SCIENCES (1947)

LABOR (1948)

POPULATION AND SOCIAL CHANGE (1949)

HIGHER EDUCATION (1950)

PUBLIC COMMUNICATION (1951)

ORGANIZATION AND MANAGEMENT (1951)

THE DEVELOPMENT OF PRE-INDUSTRIAL AREAS (1954)

AMERICAN CIVILIZATION (1954)

MEDIEVAL STUDIES (1954)

STUDIES IN CONTEMPORARY AFRICA (1956)

BUSINESS PRACTICES AND SOCIETY (1956)

CLASSICAL CIVILIZATION (1957)

MODERN EAST ASIA: CHINA (1957)

MATHEMATICAL METHODS IN THE SOCIAL SCIENCES (1959)

GENETICS AND THE EVOLUTION OF MAN (1959)

STUDIES IN THE NEW TESTAMENT (1959)

MODERN EAST ASIA: JAPAN (1960)

COMMUNISM (1960)

EIGHTEENTH CENTURY EUROPEAN CULTURE (1962)

ORIENTAL THOUGHT AND RELIGION (1962)

THE ATLANTIC COMMUNITY (1962)

THE CITY (1962)

TECHNOLOGY AND SOCIAL CHANGE (1962)

BASIC AND APPLIED SOCIAL RESEARCH (1963)

HISTORY OF LEGAL AND POLITICAL THOUGHT (1963)

THEORY OF LITERATURE (1964)

ECOLOGICAL SYSTEMS AND CULTURAL EVOLUTION (1964)

HUMAN ADAPTATION IN MODERN SOCIETY (1964)

TRADITION AND CHANGE IN SOUTH AND SOUTHEAST ASIA (1964)

ARCHAEOLOGY OF THE EASTERN MEDITERRANEAN, EASTERN EUROPE, AND THE NEAR EAST (1966)

COMPUTERS AND THEIR RELATION TO MAN AND SOCIETY (1966)

STUDIES IN MODERN ITALY (1966)

THE CHANGING METROPOLIS IN AMERICA (1967)

TRADITIONAL CHINA (1967)

BIOMATERIALS (1967)

EARLY AMERICAN HISTORY AND CULTURE (1967)

POLLUTION AND WATER RESOURCES (1967)

STUDIES IN POLITICAL AND SOCIAL THOUGHT (1968)

SLAVIC HISTORY AND CULTURE (1968)

THE STORY OF THE HEBREW BIBLE (1968)

THE NATURE OF MAN (1968)

ISRAEL AND JEWISH STUDIES (1968)

SOVIET NATIONALITY PROBLEMS (1968)

ECONOMIC HISTORY (1969)

SOCIAL AND PREVENTIVE MEDICINE (1970)

INNOVATIONS IN HIGHER EDUCATION (1970)

DEATH (1971)

PRIMITIVE AND PRE-COLUMBIAN ART (1971)

ROMANTICISM AND THE NINETEENTH CENTURY (1971)

LATIN AMERICA (1971)

KOREA (1971)

LAW AND ECONOMIC CHANGE (1971)

POPULATION BIOLOGY (1971)

POLITICAL ECONOMY OF WAR AND PEACE (1971)

THE MIDDLE EAST (1971)

APPETITIVE BEHAVIOR (1972)

THE USES OF THE OCEANS (1972)

CULTURAL PLURALISM (1972)

THE HISTORY AND PHILOSOPHY OF SCIENCE (1973)

IRISH STUDIES (1973)

CINEMA AND INTERDISCIPLINARY INTERPRETATION (1974)

INTRAUTERINE AND INFANT DEVELOPMENT (1974)

AFRICAN-AMERICAN STUDIES (1974)

WOMEN AND SOCIETY (1974)

ELITES AND POWER (1974)

STUDIES IN THE HISTORY AND CULTURE OF THE TURKS (1974)

LANGUAGE AND BEHAVIOR (1975)

DRUGS AND SOCIETY (1975)

THE HISTORY OF THE WORKING CLASS (1976)

APPENDIX 6

⫸ Festivals ⫷

Festivals are the demystificatory epiphenomena of the General Education program. They cut across the professional boundaries within the institutions and put professionals in contact with enthusiasts outside. With no concession to amateurism, the talks and performances listed below were designed to inform the audience as to current thinking on a subject, and to stimulate active discussions between the sessions. We have found the two-and three-day format successful, and append a synopsis of each.

PIERS PLOWMAN FESTIVAL

Sponsored by the Columbia University Program of General Education in The Humanities

Spring 1976
March 31–April 2

WEDNESDAY

SEMINAR: "The Value of Learning in the Quest for Salvation." Charlotte Gross; C. David Benson, University of Colorado.

LECTURE: "*Piers Plowman*: Sex and The Poet or a Riposte to Robertsonians: The Triumph of Love." C. David Benson

THURSDAY

SEMINAR: "Chaucer, Langland and The Gawain Poet: A Ricardian Study." Robert Hanning and Howard Schless, Columbia.

CLASS: Medieval Cooking Class. Lorna Sass

LECTURE: "*Piers Plowman.*" E. Talbot Donaldson, University of Indiana

FRIDAY

LECTURE: "The Historian and *Piers Plowman.*" Malcolm Bean, Columbia

LECTURE: "The Manuscripts of *Piers Plowman.*" McKay Sundwall, Columbia

LECTURE: "Langland in Context: Religious Architecture in Fourteenth-Century England." William W. Clark, Queens College

LECTURE: "A Gastronomic Tour of Richard II's Kitchen and Great Hall." Lorna Sass

CONCERT: Columbia University Collegium Musicum: Fourteenth-Century English Music. Notes by Ernest Sanders. Conductor, Paul Hawkshaw

Two cantatas by Charles Jones on *Piers Plowman*: "Anima," Nadine Herman, Soprano; "I am a Mynstral," David Smith, Tenor.

Wednesday March 22 to Friday April 2: An Exhibition of Medieval Manuscripts in the Rotunda of Low Library. Prepared by Jane Rosenthal, Barnard.

TITIAN: HIS WORLD AND HIS LEGACY
(The Bampton Lectures in America)

To commemorate the quadricentennial of the death of Titian (1576–1976) the Department of Art History and Archaeology of Columbia University, the University Program of General Education, and the Casa Italiana of Columbia University sponsored a festival in honor of the great Venetian painter. The festival was held October 15–16 at the Casa Italiana and featured a symposium, "Titian: His world and His legacy," comprising the Bampton Lectures in America for 1976–77, and a concert of Venetian music of the Renaissance.

FRIDAY

10 A.M. David Rosand, Columbia University: "Titian and the Critical Tradition."

11 A.M. James S. Ackerman, Harvard University: "Titian's Venice."

3 P.M. Patricia Labalme, Barnard College, Columbia University: "Personality and Politics in Sixteenth-Century Venice: Pietro Aretino."

4 P.M. Juergen Schulz, Brown University: "The Palaces of Titian and Pietro Aretino."

8 P.M. Concert by the Sine Nomine Singers; Harry Saltzman, conductor.

SATURDAY

10 A.M. Douglas Lewis, National Gallery of Art: "Jacopo Sansovino, Sculptor of Venice."

11 A.M. Edward Lowinsky, University of Chicago: "Music in Titian's Painting."

3 P.M. Julius S. Held, Barnard College, Columbia University (emeritus): "Titian and Rubens."

4 P.M. Theodore Reff, Columbia University: "Titian and the Venetians in Nineteenth-Century French Painting."

The papers delivered at the Titian Festival will be published by the Columbia University Press.